CONGREGATION FOR THE CLERGY

GENERAL DIRECTORY
FOR CATECHESIS

CATHOLIC TRUTH SOCIETY
PUBLISHERS TO THE HOLY SEE

This edition © 1997
The Incorporated Catholic Truth Society
192 Vauxhall Bridge Road
London SW1V 1PD
Tel.: 0171 834 4392 Fax: 0171 630 1124

ISBN 1 86082 026 3

CONTENTS

PART ONE

CATECHESIS
IN THE CHURCH'S MISSION OF EVANGELIZATION

Chapter One

Revelation and its transmission through evangelization

Chapter Two

Catechesis in the process of evangelization

Chapter Three

The nature, object and the duties of catechesis

PART TWO

THE GOSPEL MESSAGE

Chapter One

Norms and criteria
for presenting the Gospel message in catechesis

Chapter Two

"This is our faith, this is the faith of the Church"

THE CATECHISM OF THE CATHOLIC CHURCH

CATECHISMS IN THE LOCAL CHURCHES

PART THREE

THE PEDAGOGY OF THE FAITH

Chapter One

*The pedagogy of God,
source and model of the pedagogy of the faith*

Chapter Two

Elements of methodology

PART FOUR

THOSE TO BE CATECHIZED

Chapter One

Adaptation to those to be catechized: general aspects

Chapter Two

Catechesis according to age

THE CATECHESIS OF ADULTS

Chapter Two

Catechesis for special situations, mentalities and environments

Chapter Four

Catechesis in the socio-religious context

Chapter Five

Catechesis in the socio-cultural context

PART FIVE

CATECHESIS IN THE PARTICULAR CHURCH

Chapter Two

Loci and means of catechesis

Chapter Four

The organization of catechetical pastoral care in the particular Churches

ORGANIZATION AND EXERCISE OF RESPONSIBILITIES

THE CO-ORDINATION OF CATECHESIS

SOME RESPONSIBILITIES
PROPER TO THE CATECHETICAL MINISTRY

ABBREVIATIONS

I

BIBLICAL ABBREVIATIONS

Old Testament

Gen	Genesis	Mic	Micah
Ex	Exodus	Nahum	Nahum
Lev	Leviticus	Hab	Habakkuk
Num	Numbers	Zeph	Zephaniah
Deut	Deuteronomy	Hag	Haggai
Josh	Joshua	Zech	Zechariah
Judg	Judges	Mal	Malachi
Ruth	Ruth	1 Mac	1 Maccabees
1 Sam	1 Samuel	2 Mac	2 Maccabees
2 Sam	2 Samuel		

New Testament

1 Kings	1 Kings	Mt	Matthew
2 Kings	2 Kings	Mk	Mark
1 Chron	1 Chronicles	Lk	Luke
2 Chron	2 Chronicles	Jn	John
Ezra	Ezra	Acts	Acts of the Apostles
Neh	Nehemiah	Rom	Romans
Tob	Tobit	1 Cor	1 Corinthians
Jud	Judith	2 Cor	2 Corinthians
Estherd	Esther	Gal	Galatians
Job	Job	Eph	Ephesians
Ps	Psalms	Phil	Philippians
Prov	Proverbs	Col	Colossians
Eccles	Ecclesiastes	1 Thess	1 Thessalonians
Song	Song of Solomon	2 Thess	2 Thessalonians
Wis	Wisdom	1 Tim	1 Timothy
Sir	Sirach (Ecclesiasticus)	2 Tim	2 Timothy
Is	Isaiah	Tit	Titus
Jer	Jeremiah	Philem	Philemon
Lam	Lamentations	Heb	Hebrews
Bar	Baruch	Jas	James
Ezek	Ezekiel	1 Pet	1 Peter
Dan	Daniel	2 Pet	2 Peter
Hos	Hosea	1 Jn	1 John
Joel	Joel	2 Jn	2 John
Amos	Amos	3 Jn	3 John
Obad	Obadiah	Jude	Jude
Jon	Jonah	Rev	Revelation (Apocalypse)

II

DOCUMENTS OF THE MAGISTERIUM

AA   SECOND VATICAN COUNCIL, Decree on the Apostolate of the Laity, *Apostolicam Actuositatem* (18 November, 1965)

AG   SECOND VATICAN COUNCIL, Decree on missionary activity in the Church *Ad Gentes* (7 December 1965)

CA   JOHN PAUL II, Encyclical Letter *Centesimus Annus* (1 May 1991): AAS 83 (1991) pp. 793-867

CD   SECOND VATICAN COUNCIL, Decree on the pastoral office of Bishops in the Church *Christus Dominus* (28 October 1965)

CCC   *Catechism of the Catholic Church* (11 October 1992)

CCL   *Corpus Christianorum,* Latin series (Turnholt 1953 ff.)

CIC   *Codex Iuris Canonici* (25 January 1983)

ChL   JOHN PAUL II, Post-synodal Apostolic Exhortation, *Christifedeles Laici* (30 December 1988): AAS 81 (1989) pp. 393-521

COINCATI   INTERNATIONAL COUNCIL FOR CATECHESIS, *Adult Catechesis in the Christian Community,* Libreria Editrice Vaticana, 1990

CSEL   *Corpus Scriptorum Ecclesiasticorum Latinorum* (Wn 1866 ff.)

CT   JOHN PAUL II, Apostolic Exhortation *Catechesi Tradendae* (16 October 1979): AAS 71 (1979), pp. 1277-1340.

DCG (1971)   SACRED CONGREGATION FOR THE CLERGY, General Catechetical Directory, *Ad normam decreti* (11 April 1971): AAS 64 (1972). pp. 97-176

DH	SECOND VATICAN COUNCIL, Declaration on Religious Liberty, *Dignitatis Humanae* (7 December 1965)
DM	JOHN PAUL II, Encyclical Letter, *Dives in Misericordia* (30 November 1980): AAS 72 (1980) pp. 1177-1232
DV	SECOND VATICAN COUNCIL, Dogmatic Constitution on Divine Revelation *Dei Verbum* (18 November 1965)
DS	H. DENZINGER-A SCHÖNMETZER, *Enchiridion Symbolorum Definitionum et Declarationum de Rebus Fidei et Morum*, Editio XXXV, Rome 1973
EA	JOHN PAUL II, Post-synodal Apostolic Exhortation *Ecclesia in Africa* (14 September 1995): AAS 88 (1996) pp. 5-82
EN	PAUL VI, Apostolic Exhortation *Evangelii Nuntiandi* (8 December 1975): AAS 58 (1976) pp. 5-76
EV	JOHN PAUL II, Ecyclical Letter, *Evangelium Vitae* (25 March 1995): AAS 87 (1995) pp. 401-522
FC	JOHN PAUL II, Post-synodal Apostolic Exhortation *Familaris Consortio* (22 November 1981): AAS 73 (1981) pp. 81-191
FD	JOHN PAUL II, Apostolic Constitution *Fidei Depositum* (11 October 1992) AAS 86 (1994) pp. 113-118
GCM	CONGREGATION FOR THE EVAGELIZATION OF PEOPLES, *Guide for Catechists*. Document of vocational, formative and promotional orientation of Catechists in the territories depedent on the Congregation for the Evangelization of Peoples (3 December, 1993), Vatican City 1993
GE	SECOND VATICAN COUNCIL, Declaration on Education, *Gravissimum Educationis* (28 October 1965)
GS	SECOND VATICAN COUNCIL, Pastoral Constitution The Church in the Modern World. *Gaudium et Spes* (7 December 1965)

LC   COGREGATION FOR THE DOCTRINE OF THE FAITH, Instruction *Libertatis Conscientia* (22 March 1986): AAS 79 (1987) pp. 554-599

LE   JOHN PAUL II, Encyclical letter *Laborem Exercens* (14 September 1981), AAS 73 (1981), pp. 577-647

LG   SECOND VATICAN COUNCIL, Dogmatic Constitution on the Church *Lumen Gentium* (21 November 1944)

MM   JOHN XXIII, Encyclical Letter, *Mater et Magistra* (15 May 1961): AAS 53 (1961) pp. 401-464

MPD   SYNOD OF BISHOPS, Message to the People of God, *Cum iam ad exitum* on catechesis in our times (28 October 1977) Typis Polyglottis Vaticanis 1977

NA   SECOND VATICAN COUNCIL, Decree on the relationship of the Church with non-Christian Religions, *Nostra Aetate* (28 October 1965)

PB   JOHN PAUL II, Apostolic Costitution *Pastor Bonus* (28 June 1988) AAS 80 (1988), pp. 841-930

PG   *Patrologiae Cursus completus, Series Graeca* ed JACQUES P. MIGNE, Paris 1857 ff.

PL   *Patrologiae Cursus completus, Seiries Latina,* ed. JACQUES P. MIGNE, Paris 1844 ff.

PO   SECOND VATICAN COUNCIL, Decree on Priestly Life and Ministry *Presbyterorum Ordinis* (7 December 1965)

PP   PAUL VI, Encyclical Letter *Populorum Progressio* (26 March 1967) AAS 59 (1967), pp. 257-299.

RH   JOHN PAUL II, Encyclical Letter *Redemptor Hominis* (4 March 1979): AAS 71 (1979), pp. 257-324

RCIA   *Ordo Initiationis Christianae Adultorum, Rite of Christian Initiationis of Adults (R.C.I.A.)* Editio Typica, Typis Polyglottis Vaticanis 1972

RM	JOHN PAUL II, Encyclical Letter *Redemptoris Missio* (7 December 1990): AAS 83 (1991), pp. 249-340
SC	SECOND VATICAN COUNCIL, Constitution on the Sacred Liturgy *Sacrosanctum Concilium* (4 December 1963)
SYNOD 1985	SYNOD OF BISHOPS (extraordinary meeting of 1985) Final Report *Ecclesia sub verbo Dei mysteria Christi celebrans pro salute mundi* (7 December 1985), Vatican City 1985
SCh	*Sources Chrétiennes,* Collectio, Paris 1946 ff.
SRS	JOHN PAUL II, Ecyclical letter *Sollicitudo Rei Socialis* (30 December 1987) AAS 80 (1988), pp. 513-586
TMA	JOHN PAUL II, Apostolic Exhortation, *Tertio Millennio Adveniente* (10 November 1994): AAS 87 (1995) pp. 5-41
UR	SECOND VATICAN COUNCIL, Decree on Ecumenism *Unitatis Redintegratio* (21 November 1964)
UUS	JOHN PAUL II, Ecyclical Lettter *Ut Unum Sint* (25 May 1995): AAS 87 (1995) pp. 921-982.
VS	JOHN PAUL II, Encyclical Letter *Veritatis Splendor* (6 August 1993): AAS 85 (1993). pp. 1133-1228.

PREFACE

1. The Second Vatican Council prescribed that a "Directory for the catechetical instruction of the Christian people"[1] be drawn up. The Congregation for the Clergy, in execution of this conciliar mandate, availed itself of a special commission of experts, and consulted the various Episcopal Conferences, throughout the world, which made numerous suggestions and observations on the subject. The text prepared was revised by an *ad hoc* theological Commission and by the Congregation for the Doctrine of the Faith. The *General Catechetical Directory* was definitively approved by Pope Paul VI on 18 March 1971 and promulgated on 11 April 1971.

2. The thirty-year period between the conclusion of the Second Vatican Council and the threshold of the third millennium is without doubt most providential for the orientation and promotion of catechesis. It has been a time in which the evangelizing vigour of the original ecclesial community has in some ways reemerged. It has also seen a renewal of interest in the teaching of the Fathers and has made possible a return to the catechumenate. Since 1971, the General Catechetical Directory has oriented the particular Churches in their renewal of catechesis and has acted as a point of reference for content and pedagogy, as well as for methodology.

The course of catechesis during this same period has been characterized everywhere by generous dedication, worthy initiatives and by positive results for the education and growth in the faith of children, young people and adults. At the same time, however, there have been crises, doctrinal inadequacies, influ-

[1] CD 44.

ences from the evolution of global culture and ecclesial questions derived from outside the field of catechesis which have often impoverished its quality.

3.   The Magisterium of the Church, throughout these years, has never ceased to exercise its pastoral solicitude for catechesis. Numerous Bishops and Episcopal Conferences in all parts of the world have devoted considerable attention to catechesis by means of catechisms and pastoral guidelines, by promoting the formation of their priests and by encouraging catechetical research. Efforts such as these have proved fruitful and have contributed much to catechetical praxis in the particular Churches. *The Rite of Christian Initiation of Adults*, published by the Congregation for Divine Worship on 6 January 1972, has proved especially useful for catechetical renewal.

Mention must also be made in a particular way of the ministry of Pope Paul VI, who shepherded the Church in the immediate post-conciliar period. In his regard, Pope John Paul II has said: "... through his gestures, his preaching, his authoritative interpretation of the Second Vatican Council — considered by him to have been the great catechism of modern times — and through the whole of his life, my venerable predecessor Paul VI served the Church's catechesis in a particularly exemplary fashion".[2]

4.   The reflections of the General Assembly of the Synod of Bishops of October 1974 on the theme of Evangelization in the Contemporary World constitute a decisive milestone for catechesis. The propositions subsequently drawn up by the Synod were presented to Pope Paul VI, who promulgated the post-synodal Apostolic Exhortation *Evangelii Nuntiandi* of 8 December 1975. This document enunciates, amongst other things, a particularly important principle, namely, that of catechesis as a work of evan-

[2] CT 2.

gelization in the context of the mission of the Church. Henceforth catechesis would be considered as one of the enduring concerns of the Church's missionary mandate for our times.

The final General Assembly of the Synod of Bishops, convoked by Pope Paul VI in October 1977, proposed catechesis to its participants as the theme for analysis and reflection. This Synod saw "in catechetical renewal a precious gift of the Holy Spirit to the contemporary Church".[3]

5.   Taking up this catechetical heritage in 1978, Pope John Paul II set out his first orientations for catechesis in the Apostolic Exhortation *Catechesi Tradendae* of 16 October 1979. This Exhortation forms a cohesive unity with *Evangelii Nuntiandi* and fully locates catechesis within the context of evangelization.

Throughout his entire pontificate, Pope John Paul II has continually proposed a constant magisterium of the highest catechetical value. From amongst his discourses, his letters, his written teaching, particular emphasis must be given to the twelve Encyclicals, from *Redemptor Hominis* to *Ut Unum Sint*. These Encyclicals constitute in themselves a synthetic corpus of coherent doctrine with regard to the renewal of ecclesial life desired by the Second Vatican Council.

Of particular catechetical value, amongst these documents of the Petrine ministry of Pope John Paul II, the following are of special importance: *Redemptor Hominis* (4 March 1979), *Dives in Misericordia* (30 November 1980), *Dominum et Vivificantem* (18 May 1986) and *Redemptoris Missio* (7 December 1990), in which last, the permanent validity of the Church's missionary mandate is re-affirmed.

6.   On the other hand the General Assemblies of the Synod of Bishops, both ordinary and extraordinary, have been particularly

---

[3] CT 3.

important for catechesis. In this respect mention must be made of the Synods of 1980 and 1987 which dealt with the mission of the family and the vocation of the laity. Following the work of these Synods, Pope John Paul II promulgated the respective Apostolic Exhortations *Familiaris Consortio* (22 November 1981) and *Christifideles Laici* (30 December 1987). The Extraordinary Synod of Bishops of 1985 was also of decisive importance for the catechesis of our times and for the future. On that occasion, following a review of the previous twenty years of the application of the Second Vatican Council the Synodal Fathers proposed to the Holy Father a universal catechism for the Catholic Church. The proposal was most favourably received and made his own by Pope John Paul II. After a long and complex process of elaboration the *Catechism of the Catholic Church* was presented to the bishops and the Particular Churches by the Apostolic Constitution *Fidei Depositum* of the 11 October 1992.

7.   The publication of the Catechism together with the aforementioned interventions of the Magisterium necessitated a revision of the *General Catechetical Directory* so as to adapt this valuable theologico-pastoral instrument to new situations and needs. It is in service of the entire Church that the Holy See now seeks to collate this heritage and to organize it systematically in order to make it available for catechetical purposes.

The work of revising the *General Catechetical Directory* undertaken by the Congregation for the Clergy, was conducted by a group of Bishops and experts in theology and catechesis. In the revision of the General Directory, its original inspiration and content were respected. Episcopal Conferences and several experts were consulted as were the principal catechetical institutes and centres.

In its present form the *General Directory for Catechesis* seeks to arrive at a balance between two principal requirements:

– on the one hand the contextualization of catechesis in evangelization as envisaged by *Evangelii Nuntiandi;*

– on the other the appropriation of the content of the faith as presented in the *Catechism of the Catholic Church.*

8. The *General Directory for Catechesis,* while retaining the basic structure of that of 1971, is divided as follows:

– The *Introduction* takes its starting point from faith and trust in the power of the Gospel seed, and proposes guidelines for interpreting and understanding human and ecclesial conditions. These are intended to assist mission.

– *Part One* [4] has three chapters and roots catechesis above all in the conciliar Constitution *Dei Verbum,* placing it in the context of evangelization as seen in *Evangelii Nuntiandi* and *Catechesi Tradendae,* and proposes, moreover, to clarify the nature of catechesis;

– *Part Two* [5] contains two chapters, the first of which, under the title *Norms and Criteria for presenting the Gospel message in Catechesis,* puts forward afresh the entire content of the corresponding chapter of the previous text from a new and enriched perspective; the second chapter, which is completely new, serves to present the *Catechism of the Catholic Church* as a reference point for the transmission of the faith in catechesis and for the preparation of catechisms at local level; this chapter also outlines those fundamental principles to be employed in the redaction of catechisms in particular and local Churches;

– *Part Three* [6] has also been revised to formulate the main elements of a pedagogy of the faith inspired by divine pedagogy; while this question is primarily a theological one, it also involves the human sciences;

[4] Corresponds to Part II of the DCG.
[5] It has the same objectives of Part III to the DCG.
[6] Corresponds to Part IV of the DCG.

– *Part Four* [7] is entitled *Those to be catechized*; in five short chapters attention is given to the diverse situations and contexts of those to whom catechesis is directed, to matters arising from socio-religious situations, and in particular, to the question of inculturation;

– *Part Five* [8] focuses on the centrality of the particular Church and on its primordial duty to promote, organize, oversee and co-ordinate all catechetical activities; of particular significance is the description of the roles proper to the various agents involved in catechesis (who, of course, are always dependent on the Pastors of the particular Churches) and of the requirements necessary for their respective formation;

– The *Conclusion* advocates an intensification of catechetical activity in our times, and concludes with an appeal to faith in the action of the Holy Spirit and in the efficacy of the word of God sown in love.

9.   The object of this Directory is clearly the same as that pursued by the 1971 Directory. It attempts to provide those fundamental theologico-pastoral principles drawn from the Church's Magisterium, particularly those inspired by the Second Vatican Council, which are capable of better orienting and coordinating the pastoral activity of the ministry of the word and, concretely, catechesis.[9] The basic intention of the Directory was (and remains) that of offering reflections and principles, rather than im-

---

[7] Corresponds to Part V of the DCG of 1971. While several significant reasons would suggest that this section should preceed that on pedagogy, however, given the new form of Part Three it is preferred to maintain the same order as that in the 1971 text. This underlines that attention to those to whom catechesis is directed is a partipation in and a consequence of this same divine pedagogy, this Acondescenion of God in the history of Salvation (DV 13) of his self adaptation in revelation to the human condition.

[8] Assumes all the elements of Paul VI of the DCG.

[9] Cf. DCG (1971), Introduction.

mediate applications or practical directives. This method has been adopted principally for the reason that defects and errors in catechetical material can be avoided only if the nature and end of catechesis, as well as the truths and values which must be transmitted, are correctly understood from the outset.[10]

The concrete application of these principles and pronouncements by means of guidelines, national, regional or diocesan directories, catechisms and other ways deemed suitable for the effective promotion of catechesis is something which pertains to the specific competence of the various Episcopates.

10. It is evident that not all parts of the Directory have the same importance. Those dealing with Divine Revelation, the nature of catechesis, the criteria governing the proclamation of the Gospel message are universally valid. Those, however, referring to present circumstances, to methodology and to the manner of adapting catechesis to diverse age groups and cultural contexts are to be understood rather as indications or guidelines.[11]

11. The Directory is addressed principally to the Bishops, Episcopal Conferences and, in a general way, in accordance with their competence, to those who have responsibility for catechesis. Clearly it will be of use in forming those preparing for ordination to the Priesthood, in the continuing formation of priests and in the formation of catechists.

The immediate end of the Directory is to assist in the composition of catechetical directories and catechisms. Numerous notes and references have been included in this Directory, at the suggestion of many Bishops, which may be useful in drawing up such catechetical aids.

---

[10] Cf. *ibidem*.
[11] Cf. *ibidem*.

12.   Since the Directory is intended for the use of particular Churches, whose pastoral needs vary greatly, it is obvious that only common or intermediate concerns could be taken into account. This is true also of the sections dealing with the organization of catechesis at different levels. Due note should be made of this observation while using the Directory. As has been already noted in the 1971 Directory, what may appear insufficient in areas where catechesis and catechetical resources have reached a high standard, may perhaps seem excessive in areas where catechesis has not yet undergone such development.

13.   It is hoped that the publication of this document, testimony of the Apostolic See's solicitude for catechetical ministry, will be received and carefully studied in the context of the pastoral needs of each particular Church. It is to be hoped that it will promote future study and deepen research so as to respond to the needs of catechesis and the norms and directives of the Church's Magisterium.

Finally, brethren, pray for us, that the word of the Lord may speed on, and triumph as it did among you (2 *Thess* 3:1).

From the Vatican, 15 August 1997

SOLEMNITY OF THE ASSUMPTION
OF THE BLESSED VIRGIN MARY

✠ DARÍO CASTRILLÓN HOYOS
Archbishop Emeritus of Bucamaramga
Pro-Prefect

✠ CRESCENZIO SEPE
Titular Archbishop of Grado
Secretary

INTRODUCTION

Preaching the Gospel in the contemporary world

"Behold! A sower went out to sow. As he sowed some seed fell along the path, and the birds came and devoured it. Other seed fell on rocky ground, where it had not much soil, and immediately it sprang up, since it had no depth of soil; and when the sun rose it was scorched, and since it had no root it withered away. Other seed fell among thorns which grew up and choked it, and it yielded no grain. And other seeds fell into good soil and brought forth grain, growing up and increasing, and yielding thirty fold, sixty fold, and a hundred fold" (Mk 4:3-8).

14. The purpose of this Introduction is to foster in pastors and catechists a greater consciousness of the necessity to keep in mind the field in which the seed is sown, and to do so with the perspective of faith and mercy. The interpretation of the contemporary world presented here is obviously dependant on contingent historical circumstances.

"Behold! A sower going out to sow" (*Mk* 4,3)

15. The parable of the sower going out to sow is the source of inspiration for evangelization. The seed is the word of God (*Lk* 8:11). The sower is Jesus Christ. Two thousand years ago he proclaimed the Gospel in Palestine and sent the disciples to sow the Gospel in the world. Today, Jesus Christ, present in the Church through his Spirit, continues to scatter the word of the Father ever more widely in the field of the world. The condi-

tions of the soil into which it falls vary greatly. The Gospel "falls by the wayside" (*Lk* 4,4) when it is not really heard; it falls on "stony soil" without taking root; it falls "amongst the thorns" (*Lk* 4:2) where it is quickly choked by the cares and troubles that weigh upon the hearts of men. Nonetheless, some seed falls "on good soil" (*Mk* 4:8) that is among men and women who are open to a personal relationship with God and who are in solidarity with their neighbour. This seed brings forth fruit in great abundance. Jesus, in the parable of the sower, proclaims the Good News that the Kingdom of God is near, notwithstanding the problems in the soil, the tensions, conflicts and difficulties of the world. The Gospel seed makes fertile the history of mankind and promises a rich harvest. Jesus also cautions, however, that the word of God grows only in a well disposed heart.

Looking at the world from the standpoint of faith

16. The Church continues to sow the Gospel in God's field. Christians, in the most diverse social situations, perceive the world with the same eyes with which Jesus contemplated the society of his time. The disciple of Jesus Christ deeply shares the "joys and hopes, the sadness and the anxieties of the men today".[1] He gazes upon human history and participates in it, not only from the standpoint of reason but also from that of faith. In the light of faith the world appears at once "created and sustained by the love of the Creator, which has been freed from the slavery of sin by Christ, who was crucified and rose".[2] The Christian knows that every human event—indeed all reality—is marked by the creative activity of God which communicates goodness to all beings; the power of sin which limits and numbs

[1] GS 1.
[2] GS 2.

man; and the dynamism which bursts forth from the Resurrection of Christ, the seed renewing believers is the hope of a definitive "fulfilment".[3] A world-view not incorporating these three elements cannot be authentically Christian. Hence the importance of a catechesis capable of initiating catechumens and those to be catechized into a "theological reading of modern problems".[4]

THE FIELD THAT IS THE WORLD

17. The Church, Mother of mankind, above all, sees with profound sorrow "an innumerable multitude of men and women, children, adults and old people and unique human beings, who suffer misery".[5]

By means of catechesis, in which due emphasis is given to her social teaching, the Church[6] desires to stir Christian hearts "to the cause of justice"[7] and to a "preferential option or love for the poor",[8] so that her presence may really be light that shines and salt that cures.

Human rights

18. The Church, in her analysis of the soil of the world, is acutely conscious of everything that injures the dignity of the human person. She is aware that all human rights[9] spring from

---

[3] GS 2.
[4] SRS 35.
[5] SRS 13b; cf. EN 30.
[6] Cf. CT 29.
[7] SRS 41, cf. 1971 Documents of The Synod of Bishops, II: *"Justice in the world"* (30 Nov. 1971), III, *"The struggle for justice"*: AAS 43 (1971), pp. 935-937; and LC 77.
[8] SRS 41. Cf. ChL 42; TMA 51; CCC 2444-2448.
[9] Cf. JOHN XXIII. *Pacem in Terris* ,Encyclical Letter (11 April 1963), 9-27: AAS 55 (1963). pp. 261-270. Here are pointed out for the Church those more fundamental

this dignity, the constant object of Christian concern and commitment. For this reason, she looks beyond mere "social and economic indices" [10] to embrace also cultural and religious factors. What interests the Church is above all the integral development of the human person and of all peoples.[11] She notes with joy that "a beneficial trend is advancing and permeating peoples of the earth, making them ever more aware of the dignity of the individual" [12] Her vigorous insistence on respect for human rights and her decisive rejection of all their violations are clear expressions of that consciousness. The right to life, work, education, the foundation of a family, participation in public life, and to religious liberty are, today, demanded more than ever.

19.   In many places, however, human rights are clearly violated,[13] in apparent contradiction of the dignity proper to the human person. Such violations feed other forms of poverty beyond the material level: they contribute to a cultural and religious impoverishment which equally concerns the Church. The negation or restriction of human rights impoverishes the human person and entire peoples at least as much as, if not more than, material privation itself.[14] The evangelizing activity of the Church in this field of human rights has, as its undeniable objective, the task of revealing the inviolable dignity of every human person. In a certain sense, "it is the central and unifying task of service which the

human rights. In numbers 28-34 (AAS 55 (1963), pp. 270-273) are indicated the principal "human rights". Catechesis should pay attention to both of these perspectives.
[10] Cf. SRS 15a.
[11] Cf. PP 14; CA 29.
[12] ChL 5; cf. SRS 26b; VS 31c.
[13] Cf. ChL 5a. The Extraordinary Synod of 1985, II, D, 1.
[14] Cf. SRS 15e; CCC 2444; CA 57b.

Church, and the lay faithful in her, are called to render to the human family".[15] Catechesis must prepare them for this task.

Culture and cultures

20. The sower knows that the seed falls on specific soils and that it must absorb all the elements that enable it to bear fruit.[16] He also knows that some of these elements can prejudice the germination of the seed and indeed the very harvest itself.

The Constitution *Gaudium et Spes* underlines the importance of science and technology for the birth and development of modern culture. The scientific mentality, which derives from them, profoundly modifies "culture and ways of thinking",[17] with consequent human and religious repercussions. Modern man is deeply influenced by this scientific and experimental method.

Nevertheless, there is today a growing realization that such a mentality is incapable of explaining everything. Scientists themselves acknowledge that the rigour of experimental method must be complemented by some other method of knowing, if a profound understanding of the human being is ever to be attained. Linguistic theory, for example, shows that symbolic thought affords an approach to the mystery of the human person which would otherwise remain inaccessible. A rationalism which does not dichotomize man but which integrates his affective dimension, unifies him and gives fuller meaning to his life, is thus indispensable.

[15] ChL 37. Cf. CA 47.
[16] AG 22a.
[17] GS 5.

21.   Together with this "more universal form of culture",[18] there is a growing desire to esteem anew autochthonous cultures. The question posed by the Second Vatican Council is still valid: "What is to be done to prevent increased exchange between cultures (which ought to lead to genuine and fruitful dialogue between groups and nations) from disturbing the life of communities, overthrowing traditional wisdom and endangering the character proper to each people".[19]

– In many places there is an acute awareness that traditional cultures are being assailed by powerful external forces and by alien imitations of imported life-styles, with the result that the identity and values proper to peoples are thus being gradually eroded.

– Similarly acknowledged is the widespread influence of the communications media, which out of economic or ideological interest, often imposes a vision of life which does not respect the cultural distinctiveness of the peoples whom they address.

Thus, with inculturation, evangelization encounters one of its greatest challenges. In the light of the Gospel, the Church must appropriate all the positive values of culture and of cultures [20] and reject those elements which impede development of the true potential of persons and peoples.

Religious and moral factors

22.   Amongst the elements which make up the cultural heritage of a people, religious and moral factors are of particular interest to the sower. There is in contemporary culture a persistent spread of religious indifference: "Many however of our contem-

---

[18] GS 54.
[19] GS 56c.
[20] Cf. EN 20; CT 53.

poraries ...either do not at all perceive, or else explicitly reject, this intimate and vital bond of man to God".[21]

Atheism, understood as a negation of God, "must therefore be regarded as one of the most serious problems of our time".[22] While it can take various forms, it often appears today under the guise of secularism, which consists in an excessively autonomous view of man and of the world "according to which it is entirely self-explanatory without any reference to God".[23] In the specifically religious sphere there are signs of "a return to the sacred",[24] of a new thirst for transcendent reality and for the divine. The contemporary world acknowledges in a more comprehensive and vital way "the renewed interest in religious research".[25] Certainly this phenomenon "is not without ambiguity".[26] The widespread growth of sects and new religious movements and the revival of "fundamentalism"[27] are factors of serious concern for the Church and require careful analysis

23. The moral situation of today is on a par with its religious situation. There is an evident obscuring of the ontological truth of the human person—as though the denial of God meant an interior breakdown of the aspirations of the human being.[28] In many places this contributes to the rise of an "ethical relativism which would remove any sure moral reference point from politi-

---

[21] GS 19.
[22] *Ibid.*
[23] EN 55; cf. LC 41 and GS 19.
[24] Synod, II, A 1.
[25] ChL 4.
[26] Cf. RM 38.
[27] CA 29 and 46c.
[28] Cf. GS 36. JOHN PAUL II, in the encyclical letter *Dominum et vivificantem* (18 may 1986), n. 38: AAS 78 (1986), pp. 851-852, also establishes this connection: "The ideology of the 'death of God' easily demonstrates in its effects that on the 'theoretical and practical' levels it is the ideology of the 'death of man'".

cal and social life".[29] Evangelization encounters a privileged field
of activity in the religious and moral sphere. Indeed the primordial mission of the Church is to proclaim God and to be his
witness before the world. This involves making known the true
face of God and his loving plan of salvation for man, as it has
been revealed in Jesus Christ. To prepare such witnesses, it is
necessary for the Church to develop a profoundly religious catechesis, nourished on the Gospel, which will deepen man's encounter with God and forge a bond of permanent communion
with Him.

THE CHURCH IN THE WORLD

The faith of Christians

24.   The disciples of Jesus are scattered in the world as leaven
but, as in every age, they are not immune from the influences of
human situations. It is therefore necessary to enquire into the
current situation of the faith of Christians. Catechetical renewal,
developed in the Church over the last decades, continues to bear
very welcome fruit.[30] The catechesis of children, of young people
and of adults has given rise to a type of Christian who is conscious of his faith and who acts consistently with it in his life. In
such Christians this catechesis has encouraged:

  – a new and vital experience of God as merciful Father;

  – a more profound rediscovery of Jesus Christ, not only in
his divinity but also in his humanity;

  – a sense of co-responsibility on the part of all for the mission of the Church in the world;

[29] VS 101; cf. EV 19, 20.
[30] CT 3; cf. MPD 4.

– and a raising of consciousness with regard to the social obligations of the faith.

25. Nonetheless, in considering today's religious situation, the Church is also obliged to take into account the extent to which Christians "have been shaped by the climate of secularism and ethical relativism." [31] A prime category requiring examination is that of the "many people who have been baptized but lead lives entirely divorced from Christianity".[32] This in fact constitutes a mass of "non-practising Christians" [33] even though in many hearts religious feeling has not been completely lost. Re-awakening these to the faith is a real challenge for the Church. Then there are "the simple people" [34] who express themselves, at times with sincere religious feeling and deep rooted "popular devotion".[35] They possess a certain faith, "but know little even of its fundamental principles".[36] There are, moreover, numerous other Christians, often highly educated, whose religious formation amounts solely to that which they received in childhood. These also need to re-examine and develop their faith "from a different standpoint".[37]

26. There is also a certain number of baptized Christians who, desiring to promote dialogue with various cultures and other religious confessions, or on account of a certain reticence on their part to live in contemporary society as believers, fail to give explicit and courageous witness in their lives to the faith of Jesus Christ. These concrete situations of the Christian faith call ur-

---

[31] TMA 36b; GS 19c.
[32] EN 52. Cf. CT 19 and 42.
[33] EN 56.
[34] EN 52.
[35] EN 48; cr. CT 54; ChL 34b; 1985 Synod, II, A, 4; DCG (1971), 6.
[36] EN 52.
[37] Cf. EN 52; CT 44.

gently on the sower to develop *a new evangelization*,[38] especially in those Churches of long-standing Christian tradition where secularism has made greater inroads. In this new context of evangelization, missionary proclamation and catechesis, especially of the young and of adults, is an evident priority.

The internal life of the ecclesial community

27.   It is important to consider also the very life of the ecclesial community which is its innermost quality. Firstly, it is necessary to see how the Second Vatican Council has been accepted in the Church, and how it has borne fruit. The great conciliar documents have not remained a dead letter: their effects are widely acknowledged. The four constitutions (*Sacrosanctum Concilium, Lumen Gentium, Dei Verbum* and *Gaudium et Spes*) have indeed enriched the Church. In fact:

– liturgical life is more profoundly understood as the source and summit of ecclesial life;

– the people of God has acquired a keener awareness of the "common priesthood" [39] founded on Baptism, and is rediscovering evermore the universal call to holiness and a livelier sense of mutual service in charity;

– the ecclesial community has acquired a livelier sense of the word of God. Sacred Scripture, for example, is read, savoured and meditated upon more intensely;

– the mission of the Church in the world is perceived in a new way: on the basis of interior renewal, the Second Vatican Council has opened Catholics to the demands of evangelization as necessarily linked to dialogue with the world, to human development, to different cultures and religions as well as to the urgent quest for Christian unity.

[38] ChL, 34b; 33d.
[39] LG 10.

28. It must be recognized, however, that in the midst of this richness there also occur "difficulties about the acceptance of the Council".[40] Despite so comprehensive and profound an ecclesiology, the sense of belonging to the Church has weakened and "a certain disaffection towards the Church is frequently noted".[41] Thus the Church is often regarded in a one-dimensional way as a mere institution and deprived of her mystery. In some instances tendentious positions have been adopted and set in opposition to the interpretation and application of the renewal sought in the Church by the Second Vatican Council. Such ideologies and conduct have led to divisions which damage that witness of communion indispensable to evangelization. The evangelizing activity of the Church, catechesis included, must tend all the more decisively toward solid ecclesial cohesion. To this end it is urgent that an authentic ecclesiology of communion,[42] be promoted and deepened in order to arouse in Christians a deep ecclesial spirituality.

The situation of catechesis: its vitality and difficulties

29. The vitality of catechesis in recent years has been amply demonstrated by many positive aspects. Amongst others the following must be highlighted:

– the great number of priests, religious and laity who devote themselves with enthusiasm to catechesis, one of the most important ecclesial activities.

– the missionary character of contemporary catechesis and its ability to secure adherence to the faith on the part of catechu-

---

[40] Synod, 1985, I, 3.
[41] *Ibid.*
[42] CONGREGATION FOR THE DOCTRINE OF THE FAITH, Letter *Communionis notio* (28 May 1992), n. 1, AAS 85 (1993), p. 838; cf. TMA 36e.

mens and those to be catechized in a world in which religious sense is obscured must also be underlined: in this dynamic there is an acute awareness that catechesis must have a catechumenal style, as of integral formation rather than mere information; it must act in reality as a means of arousing true conversion; [43]

– consonant with what has been said, concerning the expanding role of adult catechesis [44] the catechetical programmes of many particular Churches assume extraordinary importance. This option appears to be a priority in the pastoral planning of many dioceses, and also plays a central role in many ecclesial groups and movements;

– promoted no doubt by recent directions of the Magisterium, catechetical thought, has gained much in our times in terms of quality and profundity. In this sense many local Churches already have at their disposal suitable and opportune pastoral programmes.

30.   It is necessary, however, to examine with particular attention some problems so as to identify their solutions:

– the first concerns the conception of catechesis as a school of faith, an initiation and apprenticeship in the entire Christian life of which catechists do not yet have a full understanding.

– with regard to the fundamental direction of catechesis, catechetical activity is still usually impregnated with the idea of 'Revelation': however, the conciliar concept of 'Tradition' is much less influential as an inspiration for catechesis: in much catechesis, indeed, reference to Sacred Scripture is virtually exclusive and unaccompanied by sufficient reference to the Church's long

---

[43] Cf. CT 19b.
[44] Cf. CT 43.

experience and reflection,[45] acquired in the course of her two-thousand-year history. The ecclesial nature of catechesis, in this case, appears less clearly; the inter-relation of Sacred Scripture, Tradition and the Magisterium, each according to "its proper mode" [46] does not yet harmoniously enrich a catechetical transmission of the faith;

– Concerning the object of catechesis, which always seeks to promote communion with Jesus Christ, it is necessary to arrive at a more balanced presentation of the entire truth of the mystery of Christ. Often, emphasis is given only to his humanity without any explicit reference to his divinity; at other times, less frequently today, emphasis is so exclusively placed on his divinity that the reality of the mystery of the Incarnate Word is no longer evident; [47]

– Various problems exist with regard to the content of catechesis: there are certain doctrinal *lacunae* concerning the truth about God and man; about sin and grace and about eschatology; there is a need for a more solid moral formation; presentations of the history of the Church are inadequate; and too little importance is given to her social teaching; in some regions there has been a proliferation of catechisms and texts, the products of particular initiatives whose selective tendencies and emphases are so differing as to damage that convergence necessary for the unity of the faith; [48]

– "Catechesis is intrinsically bound to every liturgical and sacramental action" [49] Frequently however, the practice of catechetics testifies to a weak and fragmetary link with the liturgy:

---

[45] Cf. CT 27b.
[46] DV 10c.
[47] Cf. CT 29b.
[48] Cf. CT 30.
[49] CT 23.

limited attention to liturgical symbols and rites, scant use of the liturgical fonts, catechetical courses whith little or no connection with the liturgical year; the marginalization of liturgical celebrations in catechetical programs;

– Concerning pedagogy, after a period in which excessive insistence on the value of method and techniques was promoted by some, sufficient attention is still not given to the demands and to the originality of that pedagogy which is proper to the faith. It remains easy to fall into a 'content-method' dualism, with resultant reductionism to one or other extreme; with regard to the pedagogical dimension the requisite theological discernment has not always been exercised; [50]

– Regarding differences between cultures in the service of the faith, it is difficult to know how to transmit the Gospel within the cultural horizons of the peoples to whom it is proclaimed, in such a way that it can be really perceived as Good News for the lives of people and of society; [51]

– Formation for the apostolate and for mission is one of the fundamental tasks of catechesis. Neverthless while there is a new sensitivity to the formation of the laity for Christian witness, for inter religious dialogue, and for their secular obligations, education for missionary activity "ad gentes" still seems weak and inadequate. Frequently, ordinary catechesis gives only marginal and inconsistent attention to the missions.

THE SOWING OF THE GOSPEL

31.   Having tested the ground, the sower sends out his workers to proclaim the Gospel through all the world and to that end shares with them the power of his Spirit. At the same time he

[50] Cf. CT 58.
[51] EN 63.

shows them how to read the signs of the times and asks of them that special preparation which is necessary to carry out the sowing.

How to read the signs of the times

32. The voice of the Spirit, which Jesus, on behalf of the Father, has communicated to his disciples "resounds in the very events of history".[52] Behind the changing data of present situations and in the deep motives of evangelization, it is necessary to discover "what may be genuine signs of the presence or the purpose of God".[53]

Such analysis, however, must always be done in the light of faith. Availing herself of the human sciences,[54] which are always necessary, the Church seeks to discover the meaning of the present situation within the perspective of the history of salvation. Her judgements on reality are always a diagnosis of the need for mission.

Some challenges for catechesis

33. In order to express its vitality and to be efficacious, catechesis today needs to undertake the following challenges and directions:

– Above all it needs to present itself as a valid service to evangelization of the Church with an accent on missionary character;

– It should address itself to those who have been and continue to be its privileged recipients: children, adolescents, young people and adults;

[52] FC 4b; cf. ChL 3e.
[53] GS 11; cf. GS 4.
[54] Cf. GS 62; FC 5.

– Based on the example of catechesis in the patristic era, it needs to form the personality of the believer and therefore be a true and proper school of Christian pedagogy;

– It needs to announce the essential mysteries of Christianity, promoting the trinitarian experience of life in Christ as the center of the life of faith;

– It needs to consider as its primary task the preparation and formation of catechists in the deep riches of the faith.

PART I

CATECHESIS IN THE CHURCH'S MISSION OF EVANGELIZATION

Catechesis
in the Church's mission of evangelization

"Go into all the world; and preach the Gospel to the whole creation" (Mk 16:15).

"Go, therefore make disciples of all nations; baptizing them in the name of the Father, and of the Son and of the Holy Spirit, teaching them to observe all that I have commanded you" (Mt 28:19-20).

"You are witnesses of these things" (Lk 24:48); "But you shall receive power when the Holy Spirit has come upon you, and you shall be my witnesses... to the end of the earth" (Acts 1:8).

The missionary mandate of Jesus

34.   Jesus Christ, after his Resurrection together with the Father sent the Holy Spirit in order that he might accomplish from within the work of salvation and that he might animate his disciples to continue the mission to the whole world.

He was the first and supreme evangelizer. He proclaimed the Kingdom of God,[1] as the urgent and definitive intervention of God in history, and defined this proclamation *"the Gospel"*, that is, the Good News. To this Gospel, Jesus devoted his entire earthly life: he made known the joy of belonging to the Kingdom,[2] its demands, its *magna carta*,[3] the mysteries which it em-

---

[1] Cf. *Mk* 1:15 and parallels. RM 12-20; CCC 541-560.
[2] Cf. *Mt* 5:3-12.
[3] Cf. *Mt* 5,1-7,29.

braces,[4] the life of fraternal charity of those who enter it[5] and its future fulfilment.[6]

The meaning and purpose of Part One

35. This first part intends to define the proper character of catechesis. Its first chapter, with regard to theology, recalls briefly the concept of Revelation as set forth in the conciliar constitution Dei Verbum. It determines in a specific manner the way in which the ministry of the word is to be conceived. The concepts *word of God, Gospel, Kingdom of God, and Tradition,* in this dogmatic constitution, are fundamental to the meaning of catechesis. Together with these, the concept of evangelization is an indispensable point of reference for catechesis. The same dynamic is presented with new and profound precision in the Apostolic Exhortation *Evangelii Nuntiandi.*

The second chapter situates catechesis within the context of evangelization and relates it to other forms of the ministry of the word of God. Thanks to this rapport one more easily discovers the proper character of catechesis.

The third chapter presents a more direct analysis of catechesis in itself: its ecclesial nature, its binding objective of communion with Jesus Christ, its tasks and the catechumenal idea by which it is inspired.

The term catechesis has undergone a semantic evolution during the twenty centuries of the Church's history. In this Directory the concept of catechesis takes its inspiration from the postconciliar Magisterial documents, principally from *Evangelii Nuntiandi, Catechesi Tradendae and Redemptoris Missio.*

---

[4] Cf. *Mt* 13:11.
[5] Cf. *Mt* 18:1-35.
[6] Cf. *Mt* 24:1-25,46.

The concept of catechesis which one has, profoundly conditions the selection and organization of its contents *(cognitive, experiential, behavioural)*, identifies those to whom it is addressed and defines the pedagogy to be employed in accomplishing its objectives.

CHAPTER I

Revelation and its transmission through evangelization

"Blessed be the God and Father of Our Lord Jesus Christ, who has blessed us in Christ with every spiritual blessing in the heavenly places... for he has made known to us in all wisdom and insight the mystery of his will, according to his purpose which he set forth in Christ as a plan for the fullness of time, to unite all things in him, things in heaven and things on earth" (Eph 1:3-10).

The revelation of God's providential plan

36. "God who creates and conserves all things by his Word, offers to men a constant evidence of himself in created things".[1] Man, who by his nature and his vocation is capable of knowing God, when he listens to this message of creation is able to arrive at the certainty of the existence of God, as the cause and end of all things and as the one who is able to reveal himself to man.

The Constitution *Dei Verbum* of the Second Vatican Council describes Revelation as that act by which God manifests himself personally to man. God truly reveals himself as one who desires to communicate himself, making the human person a participant in his divine nature.[2] In this way God accomplishes his plan of love.

---

[1] DV 3.
[2] Cf. *2 Pet* 1:4; CCC 51-52.

"It pleased God, in his goodness and wisdom, to reveal himself and to make known the mystery of his will [to men]...in order to invite and receive them into communion with himself".[3]

37. The "providential plan"[4] of the Father, fully revealed in Jesus Christ, is realized by the power of the Holy Spirit. This implies:

– the Revelation of God, of his "innermost truth",[5] of his "secret",[6] of the true vocation and dignity of the human person;[7]

– the offer of salvation to all men, as a gift of God's grace and mercy,[8] which implies freedom from evil, sin and death;[9]

– the definitive call to gather into the family of God all of his scattered children, thus realizing a fraternal union amongst men.[10]

Revelation: deeds and words

38. God, in his greatness, uses a pedagogy[11] to reveal himself to the human person: he uses human events and words to communicate his plan; he does so progressively and in stages,[12] so as to draw even closer to man. God, in fact, operates in such a manner that man comes to knowledge of his salvific plan by means of the events of salvation history and the inspired words which accompany and explain them.

[3] DV 2.
[4] *Eph* 1:9.
[5] DV 2.
[6] EN 11.
[7] Cf. GS 22a.
[8] Cf. *Eph* 2:8; EN 27.
[9] Cf. EN 9.
[10] Cf. *Gen* 11:52; AG 2b and 3a.
[11] Cf. St Irenaeus of Lyons, *"Adversus haereses"* III, 20, 2. SCh 211, 389-393. DV 15; CT 58; ChL 61; CCC 53 and 122; and also Part III, chap. 1.
[12] CCC 54-64.

"This economy of Revelation is realized by deeds and words, which are intrinsically bound up with each other. As a result,

– the works performed by God in the history of Salvation show forth and bear out the doctrine and realities signified by the words,

– the words, for their part, proclaim the works, and bring to light the mystery they contain".[13]

39.   Evangelization too which transmits Revelation to the world, is also brought about in words and deeds. It is at once testimony and proclamation, word and sacrament, teaching and task. Catechesis, for its part, transmits the words and deeds of Revelation; it is obliged to proclaim and narrate them and, at the same time, to make clear the profound mysteries they contain. Moreover, since Revelation is a source of light for the human person, catechesis not only recalls the marvels worked by God in the past, but also, in the light of the same Revelation, it interprets the signs of the times and the present life of man, since it is in these that the plan of God for the salvation of the world is realized.[14]

Jesus Christ: mediator and fullness of Revelation

40.   God revealed himself progressively to man, through the prophets and through salvific events, until he brought to completion his self-revelation by sending his own Son: [15]

"[Jesus Christ] completed and perfected Revelation, he did this by way of his presence and self manifestation—by words and works, signs and miracles, but above all by his death and glorious resurrection from the dead, and finally by sending the Spirit of truth".[16]

[13] DV 2.
[14] Cf. DCG (1971) 11b.
[15] Cf. *Heb* 1:1-2.
[16] DV 4.

Jesus Christ is not merely the greatest of the prophets but is the eternal Son of God, made man. He is, therefore, the final event towards which all the events of salvation history converge.[17] He is indeed "the Father's one, perfect and unsurpassable Word".[18]

41. The ministry of the word must always give prominence to this wonderful characteristic, proper to the economy of Revelation: the Son of God enters human history, assumes human life and death, and brings about the new and definitive covenant between God and man. It is the task of catechesis to show who Jesus Christ is, his life and ministry, and to present the Christian faith as the following of his person.[19] Consequently, it must base itself constantly on the Gospels, which "are the heart of all the Scriptures 'because they are our principal source for the life and teaching of the Incarnate Word, our Saviour'".[20]

The fact that Jesus Christ is the fullness of Revelation is the foundation for the "Christocentricity" [21] of catechesis: the mystery of Christ, in the revealed message, is not another element alongside others, it is rather the centre from which all other elements are structured and illuminated.

The transmission of Revelation by the Church, the work of the Holy Spirit

42. The Revelation of God, culminating in Jesus Christ, is destined for all mankind: "He (God) desires all men to be saved

---

[17] Cf. *Lk* 24:27.
[18] CCC 65; St John of the Cross puts it as follows: "He has told us everything at once in this one Word" (*"The Ascent of Mount Carmel"* 2,22; cf. The Liturgy of Hours, I, Office of Readings for Monday of the Second week of Advent).
[19] Cf. CT 5; CCC 520 and 2053.
[20] CCC 125, which refers to DV 18.
[21] CT 5. The Theme of Christocentrism, is explained in "The object of catechesis: communion with Jesus Christ" (Part I Chapter 3) and in "The Christocentricity of the Gospel Message (Part II, Chapter 1).

and to come to the knowledge of the truth" (*1 Tim* 2,4) [22] In virtue of his universal salvific will, God has ordained that Revelation should be transmitted to all peoples and to all generations and should remain always in its entirety.

43. To fulfil this divine plan, Jesus Christ founded the Church, built on the Apostles. He gave them the Holy Spirit from the Father and sent them to preach the Gospel to the whole world. The Apostles, by words, deeds and writings, faithfully discharged this task. [23]

This Apostolic Tradition is perpetuated in the Church by means of the Church herself. The entire Church, pastors and faithful, is responsible for its conservation and transmission. The Gospel is conserved whole and entire in the Church: the disciples of Jesus Christ contemplate it and meditate upon it unceasingly; they live it out in their everyday lives; they proclaim it in their missionary activity. As the Church lives the Gospel she is continually made fruitful by the Holy Spirit. The Spirit causes her to grow constantly in her understanding of the Gospel, prompts her and sustains the task of proclaiming the Gospel in every corner of the world. [24]

44. The integral conservation of Revelation, the word of God contained in Tradition and Scripture, as well as its continuous transmission, are guaranteed in their authenticity. The Magisterium of the Church, sustained by the Holy Spirit and endowed with "the sure charism of truth", [25] exercises the function of "authentically interpreting the word of God". [26]

---

[22] Cf.DV 7.
[23] Cf. DV 7a.
[24] Cf. DV 8 and CCC 75-79.
[25] DV 10b; cf CCC 85-87.
[26] LG 448; AG 1; GS 45; cf. CCC 774-776.

45. The Church, "universal sacrament of salvation", born of the Holy Spirit, transmits Revelation through evangelization; she announces the Good News of the salvific plan of the Father and in the sacraments, communicates his Diving gifts.

To God who reveals himself is due this obedience of faith by which man adhers to the "Gospel of the grace of God". (*Acts* 20,24) with full assent of the intellect and of the will. Guided by faith, by means of the gift of the Spirit, man succeeds in attaining to contemplate and to delight in the God of love, who in Christ has revealed the riches of his glory.[27]

Evangelization [28]

46. The Church "exists in order to evangelize" [29] that is "the carrying forth of the Good News to every sector of the human race so that by its strength it may enter into the hearts of men and renew the human race".[30]

The missionary mandate of Jesus to evangelize has various aspects, all of which, however, are closely connected with each other: "proclaim", (*Mk* 16,15) *"make disciples and teach"*,[31] *"be my witnesses"*,[32] *"baptize"*,[33] *"do this in memory of me"* (*Lk* 22,19) *"love one another"* (*Jn* 15,12). Proclamation, witness, teaching, sacraments, love of neighbour: all of these aspects are the

---

[27] Cf. *Col* 1,26.
[28] Dei Verbum and the Catechism of the Catholic Church (nn. 150-175) speak of faith as a response to Revelation. In this context, for catechetical pastoral motivation, it is preferred to associate faith more with Evangelization than with Revelation in so far as the latter, in fact, reaches man normally by way of the evangelical mission of the Church.
[29] EN 14.
[30] EN 18.
[31] Cf. *Mt* 28,19-20.
[32] *Acts* 1,8.
[33] *Mt* 28,19.

means by which the one Gospel is transmitted and they constitute the essential elements of evangelization itself.

Indeed they are so important that, at times, there is a tendency to identify them with the action of evangelization. However, "no such definition can be accepted for that complex, rich and dynamic reality which is called evangelization".[34] There is the risk of impoverishing it or even of distorting it. Evangelization, on the contrary, must develop its "totality" [35] and completely incorporate its intrinsic bipolarity: witness andproclamation,[36] word and sacrament,[37] interior change and social transformation.[38] Those who evangelize have a "global vision" [39] of evangelization and identify with the overall mission of the Church.[40]

The process of evangelization

47. The Church, while ever containing in herself the fullness of the means of salvation, always operates "by slow stages".[41] The conciliar decree *Ad Gentes* clarifies well the dynamic of the process of evangelization: Christian witness, dialogue and presence in charity (11-12), the proclamation of the Gospel and the call to conversion (13), the catechumenate and Christian Initiation (14), the formation of the Christian communities through and by

---

[34] EN 17.
[35] EN 28.
[36] Cf. EN 22a.
[37] Cf. EN 47b.
[38] Cf. EN 18.
[39] EN 24d.
[40] Cf. EN 14.
[41] AG 6b.

means of the sacraments and their ministers (1518).[42] This is the dynamic for establishing and building up the Church.

48.   Accordingly, in conformity with this, evangelization must be viewed as the process by which the Church, moved by the Spirit, proclaims and spreads the Gospel throughout the entire world. Evangelization:

– is urged by *charity,* impregnating and transforming the whole temporal order, appropriating and renewing all cultures; [43]

– bears *witness* [44] *amongst peoples of the new way of being and living which characterizes Christians;*

– *proclaims explicitly the Gospel,* through "first proclamation",[45] calling to conversion.[46]

– *initiates into the faith and the Christian life,* by means of "catechesis" [47] and the "sacraments of Christian initiation",[48] those who convert to Jesus Christ or those who take up again the path of following him, incorporating both into the Christian community; [49]

– constantly nourishes the gift of *communion* [50] amongst the faithful by means of continuous education in the faith (homilies and other forms of catechesis), the sacraments and the practice of charity;

---

[42] In the dynamism of evangelization a distinction must be made between "initial situations" (*initia*), "gradual developments" (*gradus*) and situations of maturity: "appropriate acts must correspond to condition and state" (AG 6).

[43] EN 18-20 and RM 52-54; cf. AG 11-12 and 22.

[44] EN 21 and 41; RM 42-43; AG 11.

[45] EN 51,52,53. cf. CT 18, 19, 21, 25; RM 44.

[46] AG 13; EN 10 and 23; CT 19; RM 46.

[47] EN 22 and 24; CT 18; cf. AG 14 and RM 47.

[48] AG 14; CCC 1212; cf. CCC 1229-1233.

[49] EN 23; CT 24; RM 48-49; cf. AG 15.

[50] ChL 18.

– continuously arouses *mission*,[51] sending all the disciples of Christ to proclaim the Gospel, by word and deed throughout the whole world.

49. The process of evangelization,[52] consequently, is structured in stages or "essential moments": [53] missionary activity directed toward non-believers and those who live in religious indifference; initial catechetical activity for those who choose the Gospel and for those who need to complete or modify their initiation; pastoral activity directed toward the Christian faithful of mature faith in the bosom of the Christian community.[54] These moments, however, are not unique: they may be repeated, if necessary, as they give evangelical nourishment in proportion to the spiritual growth of each person or of the entire community.

The ministry of the word in evangelization

50. The ministry of the word [55] is a fundamental element of evangelization. The presence of Christianity amongst different hu-

---

[51] ChL 32, which demonstrates the close connection between "communion" and "mission".

[52] Cf. EN 24.

[53] Cf. CT 18.

[54] Cf. AG 6f; RM 33 and 48.

[55] Cf. *Acts* 6:4. The Ministry of the Word of God is fostered in the Church by:
 – the ordained ministers (cf. CIC 756-757);
 – members of institutes of consecrated life in light of their consecration to God (cf. CIC 758);
 – the lay faithful in light of their baptism and confirmation (cf. CIC 759). In regard to the term *ministry* (*servitium*), it is necessary that all reference be made to the uniqueness and to the source of all ministry which is the *ministry of Christ*. To a certain extent this applies also without ambiguity to the non-ordained faithful. In the original meaning, it expresses the work with which the members of the Church carry on the mission of Christ, both within the Church and throughout the world. However, when the term is distinguished from and compared with the various *munera and officia*, then it should be clearly noted that only in virtue of sacred ordina-

man groups and its living witness must be explained and justified by the explicit proclamation of Jesus Christ the Lord. "There is no true evangelization if the name, the teaching, the life, the promises, the Kingdom and the mystery of Jesus of Nazareth, the Son of God, are not proclaimed".[56] Those who are already disciples of Jesus Christ also require to be constantly nourished by the word of God so that they may grow in their Christian life.[57]

The ministry of the word, within the context of evangelization, transmits Revelation, through the Church, by using human words. These, however, always refer to works: to those which God has done and continues to do, especially in the liturgy; to the witness of Christians; to the transforming action which these Christians achieve, together with so many men of good will, throughout the world. This human word of the Church is the means used by the Holy Spirit to continue dialogue with humanity. He is, in fact, the principle agent of the ministry of the word, the one through whom "the living voice of the Gospel rings out in the Church—and through her in the world".[58]

The ministry of the word is exercised in "different forms".[59] The Church, since apostolic times,[60] in her desire to offer the word of God in the most appropriate manner, has realized this

---

tion does the word obtain that full, univocal meaning that tradition has attributed to it (cf. JOHN PAUL II, Allocution at the Simposium on "The Participation of the Lay Faithul in the Priestly Ministry" n. 4, L'Osservatore Romano, English Edition, 11 May 1994.

[56] EN 22; cf. EN 51-53.

[57] Cf. EN 42-45, 54, 57.

[58] DV 8c.

[59] PO 4b; cf. CD 13c.

[60] Many diverse forms of this single ministry appear in the New Testament: "Proclamation, teaching, exhortation, prophecy, witness... this richness of expression is notable.

ministry in the most varied of ways.[61] All of these, however, perform the essential and fundamental functions of the ministry of the word itself.

Functions and forms of the ministry of the word

51. The following are the principal functions of the ministry of the word:

— Called together and called to faith

This function is the most immediate expression of the missionary mandate of Jesus. It is realized through "the primary proclamation", directed to non-believers; those who have chosen unbelief, those Christians who live on the margins of Christian-life, those who follow other religions.[62] The religious awakening of the children of Christian families, is also an eminent form of this function.

— Initiation

Those who are moved by grace to decide to follow Jesus are "introduced into the life of faith, of the liturgy and of the charity of the People of God".[63] The Church achieves this function fundamentally by catechesis, in close relation with the sacraments of initiation, whether these are about to be received or have already been received. Important forms include: the catechesis of non-baptized adults in the catechumenate, the catechesis of baptized adults who wish to return to the faith, or of those who

---

[61] The forms through which the ministry of the word is filtered are not in reality intrinsic to the Christian message as though to imply that diversity of form connotes different messages. These are, rather, accentuations or tones more or less explicitated and adapted to the situation of faith of each person or group of persons in their concrete situations.

[62] EN 51-53.

[63] AG 14.

need to complete their initiation; the catechesis of children and of the young, which of itself has the character of initiation. Christian education in families and religious instruction in schools also have an initiatory function.

– *Continuous education in the faith*

In many regions this is also called "permanent catechesis".[64]

It is intended for those Christians who have been initiated in the basic elements of the Christian faith, but who need constantly to nourish and deepen their faith throughout their lives. This function is accomplished through a great variety of forms: "systematic and occasional, individual and community, organized and spontaneous".[65]

– *The liturgical function*

The ministry of the word also has a liturgical function since, when realized within the context of a sacred action, it is an integral part of that action.[66] It takes different forms but amongst them the most important is the homily. Other forms in the liturgical context include celebrations of the word and instruction received during the administration of the sacraments. On the other hand, mention must also be made of the immediate preparation

---

[64] There are different reasons which for using such expressions as "continuing education in the faith" or "continuing catechesis". They may not however, relativise the prior, basic, structural and specific character of catechesis understood as basic initiation. The expression "continuing education in the faith" has been widely used in catechetical praxis since the Second Vatican Council. It denotes a second grade of catechesis which is subject to initiatory catechesis. It does not denote the totality of catechetical activity. The distinction between basic formation and permanent formation is used in reference to priestly formation in the Apostolic Exhortation, *Pastores dabo vobis* of John Paul II, chapters five and six, especially in n. 71: AAS 84 (1992), pp. 729 ff; 778 ff; 782-783.

[65] DCG (1971) 19d.

[66] Cf. SC 35; CCC 1154.

for reception of the different sacraments, the celebration of sacramentals and above all of the participation of the faithful in the Eucharist, as a primary means of education in the faith.

– *The theological function*

This seeks to develop understanding of the faith and is to be situated in the dynamic of *"fides quaerens intellectum"*, that is, of belief which seeks to understand.[67] Theology, in order to fulfil this function, needs to confront philosophical forms of thought, various forms of humanism and the human sciences, and dialogue with them. It is articulated whenever: "the systematic treatment and the scientific investigation of the truths of the Faith" [68] are promoted.

52. The important forms of the ministry of the Word are: the first annoucement or missionary preaching, pre and post baptismal catechesis, the liturgical forms and the theological forms. Then, it often happens, for pastoral reasons, that important forms of the ministry of the word must assume more than one function. Catechesis, for example, together with its initiatory forms, has frequently to discharge tasks of mission. The same homily, depending on circumstances, can take on both the functions of convocation and of integral initiation.

Conversion and faith

53. In proclaiming the Good News of Revelation to the world, evangelization invites men and women to conversion and faith.[69] The call of Jesus, "Repent and believe in the Gospel", (*Mk* 1,15)

---

[67] Cf. CONGREGATION FOR THE DOCTRINE OF THE FAITH, *"Instruction on the ecclesial vocation of the theologian"*, Donum veritatis (24 May 1990), n. 6: AAS 82 (1990), p. 1552.

[68] DCG (1971) 17; cf. GS 62g.

[69] Cf. *Rm* 10:17; LG 16 and AG 7; cf. CCC 846-848.

continues to resound today by means of the Church's work of evangelization. The Christian faith is, above all, conversion to Jesus Christ,[70] full and sincere adherence to his person and the decision to walk in his footsteps.[71] Faith is a personal encounter with Jesus Christ making, of oneself a disciple of him. This demands a permanent commitment to think like him, to judge like him and to live as he lived.[72] In this way the believer unites himself to the community of disciples and appropriates the faith of the Church.[73]

54.   This "Yes" to Jesus Christ, who is the fullness of the revelation of the Father is twofold: a trustful abandonment to God and a loving assent to all that he has revealed to us. This is possible only by means of the action of the Holy Spirit.[74]

> "By faith man freely commits his entire self completely to God, making the full submission of his intellect and will to God who reveals, and willingly assenting to the Revelation given by him".[75]

"To believe has thus a double reference: to the person and to the truth; to the truth, by trust in the person who bears witness to it".[76]

55.   Faith involves a change of life, a *"metanoia"*,[77] that is a profound transformation of mind and heart; it causes the believer to live that conversion.[78] This transformation of life manifests itself

[70] Cf. AG 13a.
[71] Cf. CT 5b.
[72] Cf. CT 20b.
[73] Cf. CCC 166-167.
[74] Cf. CCC 150 and 176.
[75] DV 5.
[76] CCC 177.
[77] Cf. EN 10; AG 13b; CCC 1430-1431.
[78] EN 23.

at all levels of the Christian's existence: in his interior life of adoration and acceptance of the divine will, in his action, participation in the mission of the Church, in his married and family life; in his professional life; in fulfilling economic and social responsibilities.

Faith and conversion arise from the *"heart"*, that is, they arise from the depth of the human person and they involve all that he is. By meeting Jesus Christ and by adhering to him the human being sees all of his deepest aspirations completely fulfilled. He finds what he had always been seeking and he finds it superabundantly.[79] Faith responds to that *"waiting"*,[80] often unconscious and always limited in its knowledge of the truth about God, about man himself and about the destiny that awaits him. It is like pure water [81] which refreshes the journey of man, wandering in search of his home. Faith is a gift from God. It can only be born in the intimacy of Man's heart as a fruit of that "grace [which] moves and assists him",[82] and as a completely freeresponse to the promptings of the Holy Spirit who moves the heart and turns it toward God, and who "makes it easy for all to accept and believe the truth".[83] The Blessed Virgin Mary lived these dimensions of faith in the most perfect way. The Church "venerates in Mary the purest realization of faith".[84]

---

[79] Cf. AG 13.
[80] Cf. RM 45c.
[81] Cf. RM 46d.
[82] DV 5; cf. CCC 153.
[83] *Ibidem.*
[84] CCC 149.

The process of continuing conversion

56.   Faith is a gift destined to grow in the hearts of believers.[85] Adhering to Jesus Christ, in fact, sets in motion a process of continuing conversion, which lasts for the whole of life.[86] He who comes to faith is like a new born child,[87] who, little by little, will grow and change into an adult, tending towards the state of the "perfect man",[88] and to maturity in the fullness of Christ. From a theological viewpoint, several important moments can be identified in the process of faith and conversion:

a) Interest in the Gospel. The first moment is one in which, in the heart of the non believer or of the indifferent or of those who practise other religions, there is born, as a result of its first proclamation, an interest in the Gospel, yet without any firm decision. This first movement of the human spirit towards faith, which is already a fruit of grace, is identified by different terms: "propensity for the faith",[89] "evangelic preparation",[90] inclination to believe, "religious quest".[91] The Church calls those who show such concern "sympathizers".[92]

b) Conversion. This first moment of interest in the Gospel requires a period of searching[93] to be transformed into a firm option. The option for faith must be a considered and mature one. Such searching, guided by the Holy Spirit and the proclamation

---

[85] CT 20a: "It is in fact a matter of giving growth, at the level of knowledge and in life, to the seed of faith sown by the Holy Spirit with the initial proclamation".

[86] Cf. RM 46b.

[87] Cf. *1 Pet* 2:2; *Heb* 5:13.

[88] *Eph* 4:13.

[89] RCIA 12.

[90] Cf. EUSEBIUS OF CAESREA, *"Praeparatio evangelica"*, I, 1; SCh 206, 6; LG 16; AG 3a.

[91] ChL 4c.

[92] RCIA 12 and 111.

[93] Cf. RCIA 6 and 7.

of the *Kerygma,* prepares the way for conversion which is certainly "initial",[94] but brings with it adherence to Christ and the will to walk in his footsteps. This "fundamental option" is the basis for the whole Christian life of the Lord's disciple.[95]

c) Profession of faith. Abandonment of self to Jesus Christ arouses in believers a desire to know him more profoundly and to identify with him. Catechesis initiates them in knowledge of faith and apprenticeship in the Christian life, thereby promoting a spiritual journey which brings about a "progressive change in outlook and morals".[96] This is achieved in sacrifices and in challenges, as well as in the joys which God gives in abundance. The disciple of Jesus Christ is then ready to make an explicit, living and fruitful profession of faith.[97]

d) Journeying towards perfection. The basic maturity which gives rise to the profession of faith is not the final point in the process of continuing conversion. The profession of baptismal faith is but the foundation of a spiritual building which is destined to grow. The baptized, moved always by the Spirit, nourished by the sacraments, by prayer and by the practise of charity, and assisted by multiple forms of ongoing education in the faith, seeks to realize the desire of Christ: "Be perfect as your heavenly Father is perfect".[98] This is the call to the fullness of perfection which is addressed to all the baptized.

57. The ministry of the word is at the service of this process of full conversion. The first proclamation of the Gospel is characterized by the call to faith; catechesis by giving a foundation to

---

[94] AG 13b..
[95] Cf. AG 13; EN 10; RM 46; VS 66; RCIA 10.
[96] AG 13b.
[97] Cf. MPD 8b; CCC 187-189.
[98] *Mt* 5:48; cf. LG 11, 40b, 42e.

conversion and providing Christian life with a basic structure; while ongoing education in the faith, in which the place of the homily must be underlined, is characterized by being the necessary nourishment of which every baptized adult has need in order to live.[99]

Socio-religious situations and evangelization

58. The evangelization of the world finds itself placed in a very diversified and changing religious panorama, in which it is possible to distinguish three basic situations [100] requiring particular and precise responses.

a) The situation of those "peoples, groups and socio-cultural contexts in which Christ and his Gospel are not known, or which lack Christian communities sufficiently mature to be able to incarnate the faith in their own environment and proclaim it to other groups".[101] This situation requires a *"mission ad gentes"*,[102] where missionary activity is concentrated preferably toward young people and adults. Its particular characteristic consists in the fact that it is directed to non-Christians and invites them to conversion. In this context catechesis is usually developed within the baptismal catechumenate.

b) There are, moreover, situations in which, in a definite socio-cultural context, "there are Christian communities with ade-

---

[99] Cf. DV 24; EN 45.
[100] Cf. RM 33.
[101] RM 33b.
[102] RM 33b. It is important to be cognisant of the parameters (*fines*) that RM assigns to the "mission ad gentes". This is not restricted solely to territorial parameters (RM 37) but also to new social environments and phenomena (RM 37) such as large cities, youth, migration and to cultural areas and modern fora (RM 37) such as modern communications, science and ecology. In virtue of this a particular Church already rooted in a particular territory carries on a *missio ad gentes* not only *ad extra* but also *ad intra*.

quate and solid ecclesial structures. They are fervent in their faith and in Christian living. They bear witness to the Gospel in their surroundings and have a sense of commitment to the Universal mission".[103] These communities demand an intense "pastoral action of the Church" since they are made up of people and families of profound Christian outlook. In such contexts it is vital that catechesis for children, adolescents and young people develop various processes of well articulated Christian initiation which permit these to arrive at adulthood with mature faith which makes evangelizers of those who have been evagelized. Also in these situations adults are also in need of different types of Christian formation.

c) In many countries of established Christian tradition and sometimes in younger Churches there exists "an intermediate situation",[104] where "entire groups of the baptized have lost a living sense of the faith, or even no longer consider themselves members of the Church and live a life far removed from Christ and his Gospel".[105] Such situations require "a new evangelization". The peculiar nature of this situation is found in the fact that missionary activity is directed towards the baptized of all ages, who live in a religious context in which Christian points of reference are perceived purely exteriorly. Here primary proclamation and basic catechesis are priorities.

The mutual connection between the activities of evangelization which correspond to these socio-religious situations.

59. These socio-religious situations obviously differ from each other and it is wrong to regard them as equal. Such diversity,

---

[103] RM 33c.
[104] RM 33d.
[105] *Ibidem.*

which has always existed in the Church's mission, acquires in today's changing world a new significance. Indeed, increasingly different situations oftentimes co-exist in the same territory. In
many of the great cities, for example, a situation requiring *"missio ad gentes"* can co-exist along with one which requires "new
evangelization". Together with these there can be present in a
dynamic way Christian missionary communities sustained by
"comprehensive pastoral activity". Very often today, local
Churches are obliged to address the entire panorama of these religious situations. "The boundaries between pastoral care of the
faithful, new evangelization and specific missionary activity are
not clearly definable, and it is unthinkable to create barriers between them or to put them into water-tight compartments".[106] In
fact, "each of them influences, stimulates and assists the others".[107]

In order, therefore, to arrive at a mutual enrichment between
the various activities of evangelization which can co-exist, it is
useful to remember that:

– Mission *ad gentes,* regardless of the zone or context in
which it is realized, is the missionary responsibility most specifically entrusted to the Church by Jesus and thus the exemplary
model for all her missionary activity. New evangelization cannot
supplant or be substituted for 'the mission *ad gentes*,' which continues to be the paradigm and primary task of missionary activity.[108]

– "The model for all catechesis is the baptismal catechumenate when, by specific formation, an adult converted to belief is

---

[106] RM 34b.
[107] RM 34c. The text also speaks of the mutual enrichment between the mission ad
intra and the mission ad *extra*. In RM 59c, in the same way, it is shown how the
mission *ad gentes* encourages people towards development, while "new evangelization" in the more developed nations brings about a clear sense of solidarity towards others.
[108] Cf. RM 31,34.

brought to explicit profession of baptismal faith during the Paschal Vigil".[109] This catechumenal formation should inspire the other forms of catechesis in both their objectives and in their dynamism.

– "Catechesis for adults, since it deals with persons who are capable of an adherence that is fully responsible, must be considered the chief form of catechesis. All the other forms, which are indeed always necessary, are in some way oriented to it".[110] This implies that the catechesis of other age groups should have it for a point of reference and should be expressed in conjunction with it, in a coherent catechetical programme suitable to meet the pastoral needs of dioceses.

In this way catechesis, situated in the context of the Church's mission of evangelization and seen as an essential moment of that mission, receives from evangelization a missionary dynamic which deeply enriches it and defines its own identity. The ministry of catechesis appears, then, as a fundamental ecclesial service for the realization of the missionary mandate of Jesus.

[109] Synod, MPD 8.
[110] DCG (1971) 20; CT 43; cf. Part Four, chap. 2.

CHAPTER II

Catechesis
in the process of evangelization

"Things what we have heard and known, that our fathers have told us. We will not hide them from their chidren, but tell to the coming generation, the glorious deeds of the Lord, and his might, and the wonders he has wrought" (Ps 78:3-4).

"He (Apollos) had been instructed in the Way of the Lord and being fervent in spirit he spoke and taught accurately in the things concerning Jesus" (Acts 18:25).

60.   In this chapter the relationship of catechesis with the other elements of evagelization, of which it is itself an integral part, is demonstrated. Thus, firstly, the relationship of catechesis with the primary proclamation, which is realized in mission, is described. There follows an examination of the close connection between catechesis and the sacraments of Christian initiation. Then is perceived the fundamental role of catechesis in the ordinary life of the Church and its role as continuing teacher in the faith. Special consideration is given to the relationship between catechesis and the teaching of religion in schools, since both activities are profoundly inter-connected, and, together with education in the Christian home, are basic to the formation of children and young people.

Primary or first proclamation and catechesis

61.   Primary proclamation is addressed to non-believers and those living in religious indifference. Its functions are to proclaim

the Gospel and to call to conversion. Catechesis, "distinct from the primary proclamation of the Gospel",[1] promotes and matures initial conversion, educates the convert in the faith and incorporates him into the Christian community. The relationship between these two forms of the ministry of the word is, therefore, a relationship of complementary distinction. Primary proclamation, which every Christian is called to perform, is part of that *"Go"* [2] which Jesus imposes on his disciples: it implies, therefore, a going-out, a haste, a message. Catechesis, however, starts with the condition indicated by Jesus himself: "whosoever believes",[3] whosoever converts, whosoever decides. Both activities are essential and mutually complementary: go and welcome, proclaim and educate, call and incorporate.

62.   Nevertheless in pastoral practice it is not always easy to define the boundaries of these activities. Frequently, many who present themselves for catechesis truly require genuine conversion. Because of this the Church usually desires that the first stage in the catechetical process be dedicated to ensuring conversion.[4] In the *"missio ad gentes"*, this task is normally accomplished during the 'pre-catechumenate'.[5] In the context of "new evangelization" it is effected by means of a "kerygmatic catechesis", sometimes called "pre-catechesis", [6] because it is based on the precatechumenate and is proposed by the Gospel and directed towards a solid option of faith. Only by starting with conver-

[1] CT 19.
[2] *Mk* 16:15 and *Mt* 28:19.
[3] *Mk* 16:16.
[4] Cf. CT 19; DCG (1971) 18.
[5] RCIA 9-13. cf. CIC 788.
[6] In the present directory it is supposed that those to whom *kerygmatic catechesis* or *pre-catechesis* is addressed will be interested in the Gospel. In situations where they have no such interest then primary proclamation is called for.

sion, and therefore by making allowance for the interior disposition of "whoever believes", can catechesis, strictly speaking, fulfil its proper task of education in the faith.[7]

The fact that catechesis, at least initially, assumes a missionary objective, does not dispense a particular Church from promoting an institutionalized programme of primary proclamation to execute more directly Jesus's missionary command. Catechetical renewal should be based thus on prior missionary evangelization.

CATECHESIS AT THE SERVICE OF CHRISTIAN INITIATION

Catechesis, an essential "moment" in the process of evangelization

63.   The Apostolic Exhortation *Catechesi Tradendae* places catechesis firmly within the Church's mission and notes that evangelization is a rich, complex and dynamic reality which comprises essential but different "moments". "Catechesis", it adds, "is one of these moments—a very remarkable one—in the whole process of evangelization".[8] This is to say that there are activities which "prepare"[9] for catechesis and activities which "derive" from it[10] The "moment" of catechesis is that which corresponds to the period in which conversion to Jesus Christ is formalized, and provides a basis for first adhering to him. Converts, by means of "a period of formation, an apprenticeship in the whole Christian life",[11] are initiated into the mystery of salvation and an evangelical style of life. This means "initiating the hearers into the fullness of Christian life".[12]

---

[7] Cf. RCIA 9,10,50; CT 19.
[8] CT 18; cf CT 20c.
[9] CT 18.
[10] *Ibidem.*
[11] AG 14.
[12] CT 18.

64. In discharging in different ways the initiatory function of the ministry of the word, catechesis lays the foundation for the building of the faith.[13] Other functions of the same ministry will continue to build, at different levels, on that foundation.

Initiatory catechesis is thus the necessary link between missionary activity which calls to faith and pastoral activity which continually nourishes the Christian community. This is not, therefore, an optional activity, but basic and fundamental for building up the personality of the individual disciple, as it is for the whole Christian community. Without it, missionary activity lacks continuity and is sterile, while pastoral activity lacks roots and becomes superficial and confused: any misfortune could cause the collapse of the entire building.[14]

In truth, "the inner growth [of the Church] and her correspondence with God's plan depend essentially on catechesis".[15] In this sense catechesis must always be considered a priority in evangelization.

Catechesis, at the service of Christian initiation

65. Faith, by means of which man responds to the proclamation of the Gospel, requires Baptism. The close connection between the two realities is rooted in the will of Christ himself, who commanded his apostles to make disciples of all nations and to baptize them. "The mission to baptize, and so the sacramental mission, is implied in the mission to evangelize".[16]

Those who have converted to Jesus Christ and who have been educated in the faith by means of catechesis, by receiving the sacraments of Christian initiation (Baptism, Confirmation and

[13] St CYRIL OF JERUSALEM, *Catecheses illuminandorum*, I, 11; PG. 33, 351-352.
[14] Cf. *Mt* 7:24-27.
[15] CT 13; cf. CT 15.
[16] CCC 1122.

Eucharist) "are delivered from the powers of darkness through the sacraments of Christian initiation and having died, been buried, and risen with Christ, they receive the Spirit of adoption as children and celebrate with the whole people of God the memorial of the Lord's death and resurrection".[17]

66. Catechesis, is thus, a fundamental element of Christian initiation and is closely connected with the sacraments of initiation, especially with Baptism, "the sacrament of faith".[18] The link uniting catechesis and Baptism is true profession of faith, which is at once an element inherent in this sacrament and the goal of catechesis. The aim of catechetical activity consists in precisely this: to encourage a living, explicit and fruitful profession of faith.[19] The Church, in order to achieve this, transmits to catechumens and those to be catechized, her living experience of the Gospel, her faith, so that they may appropriate and profess it. Hence, "authentic catechesis is always an orderly and systematic initiation into the revelation that God has given of himself to humanity in Christ Jesus, a revelation stored in the depths of the Church's memory and in Sacred Scripture, and constantly communicated from one generation to the next by a living active *traditio*".[20]

---

[17] AG 14. Cf. CCC 1212, 1229.

[18] CCC 1253. In the baptismal catechumenate of adults in the mission *ad gentes* catechesis precedes Baptism. In the catechesis of the baptized, formation is subsequent to Baptism. However, also in this case a function of catechesis is to help to discover and bring to life the immense richness of Baptism already received. CCC 1231 uses the expression *post-baptismal catechumenate*. ChL 61 calls it post-baptismal catechesis.

[19] Cf. CCC 1229; CD 14.

[20] CT 22. Cf. CT 21b, 18d.

Fundamental characteristics of initiatory catechesis

67.   Catechesis acquires certain characteristics in virtue of being an "essential moment" in the process of evangelization, in the service of Christian initiation.[21] It is:

– a comprehensive and systematic formation in the faith. The Synod of 1977 underscored the need for a "comprehensive and structured" [22] catechesis, since catechesis is principally distinguished from other forms of presenting the word of God by its comprehensive and vital deepening of the mystery of Christ;

– this comprehensive formation includes more than instruction: it is an apprenticeship of the entire Christian life, it is a "complete Christian initiation",[23] which promotes an authentic following of Christ, focused on his Person; it implies education in knowledge of the faith and in the life of faith, in such a manner that the entire person, at his deepest levels, feels enriched by the word of God; it helps the disciple of Christ to transform the old man in order to assume his baptismal responsibilities and to profess the faith from the "heart"; [24]

– a basic and essential formation,[25] centred on what constitutes the nucleus of Christian experience, the most fundamental certainties of the faith and the most essential evangelical values; it lays the foundation of the spiritual edifice of the Christian,

---

[21] Cf. CT 21.

[22] Two things need to be underlined in this synodal contribution taken from *Catechesi Tradendae:* the preoccupation to take into account a pastoral problem ("I insist on the necessity of an organic and systematic Christian education because for diverse reasons there has been a tendency to minimize its importance"), and the fact of considering the organic nature of catechesis as the *principal characteristic* connoting it.

[23] CT 21.

[24] Cf. CT 20; St Augustine, *De catechizandis rudibus,* I, chap. 4, n. 8; CCL 46, 128-129.

[25] Cf. CT 21b.

nurtures the roots of his faith life and enables him to receive more solid nourishment in the ordinary life of the Christian community.

68. In summary, initiatory catechesis, being comprehensive and systematic, cannot be reduced to the circumstantial or the occasional.[26] As it is formation for the Christian life it comprises but surpasses mere instruction.[27] Being essential, it looks to what is "common" for the Christian, without entering into disputed questions nor transforming itself into a form of theological investigation. Finally, being initiatory, it incorporates into the community, which lives, celebrates and bears witness to the faith. It fulfils, at once, initiatory, educational and instructional functions.[28] This inherent richness in the Catechumenate of non-baptized adults should serve to inspire other forms of catechesis.

CATECHESIS AT THE SERVICE OF ONGOING FORMATION IN THE FAITH

Continuing education in faith within the Christian community

69. Continuing or on-going education in the faith follows upon basic education and presupposes it. Both fulfil two distinct but complementary functions of the ministry of the word while serving the process of continuing conversion. Initiatory catechesis lays the basis for the Christian life of the followers of Jesus. The process of continuing conversion goes beyond what is provided by basic catechesis. In order to encourage this process, it is necessary to have a Christian community which welcomes the initiated, sustains them and forms them in the faith: "Catechesis runs

[26] Cf. CT 21c.
[27] Cf. CT 33 and CCC 1231; AG 14.
[28] Cf. DCG (1971) 31.

the risk of becoming barren if no community of faith and Christian life welcomes the catechumen at a certain stage of his catechesis".[29] The accompaniment which a community gives to the initiated is eventually transformed into their being totally integrated by the same community.

70.   In the Christian community the disciples of Jesus Christ are nourished at a twofold table; "that of the word of God and that of the Body of Christ".[30] The Gospel and the Eucharist are the constant food for the journey to the Father's House. The action of the Holy Spirit operates so that the gift of "communion" and the task of "mission" are deepened and lived in an increasingly intense way.

Continuing formation in the faith is directed not only to the individual Christian, to accompany them in their journey towards holiness, but also to the Christian community as such so that it may mature also in its interior life of love of God and of the brethren as well as in its openness to the world as a missionary community. The desire of Jesus and his prayer to the Father are an unceasing appeal: "May they all be one; even as thou, Father, art in me, and I in thee, that they may also be in us, so that the world may believe that thou hast sent me".[31] Approaching this ideal, little by little, demands of the community a great fidelity to the action of the Holy Spirit, the constant nourishment of the Body and Blood of Christ and continuing education in the faith, listening all the time to the word.

At this table of the word of God, the homily occupies a privileged position, since it "takes up again the journey of faith put forward by catechesis and brings it to its natural fulfilment, at

---

[29] CT 24.
[30] DV 21.
[31] *Jn* 17:21.

the same time it encourages the Lord's disciples to begin anew each day their spiritual journey in truth, adoration and thanksgiving".[32]

Various forms of continuing catechesis

71. For continuing education in the faith, the ministry of the word uses many forms of catechesis. Among these the following may be highlighted:

– The study and exploration of Sacred Scripture, read not only in the Church but with the Church and her living faith, which helps to discover divine truth, which it contains, in such a way as to arouse a response of faith.[33] The *"lectio divina"* is an eminent form of this vital study of Scripture.

– A Christian reading of events, which is required of the missionary vocation of the Christian community. In this respect the study of the social teaching of the Church is indispensable, since "its main aim is to interpret these realities, determining their conformity with or divergence from the lines of the Gospel teaching".[34]

– Liturgical catechesis, prepares for the sacraments by promoting a deeper understanding and experience of the liturgy. This explains the contents of the prayers, the meaning of the signs and gestures, educates to active paricipation, contemplation

[32] Cf. CT 48; cf. SC 52; DV 24; DCG (1971) 17; *Missale Romanum, Ordo Lectionum Missae*, n. 24 Editio Typica Altera, Libreria Editrice Vaticana 1981.

[33] Cf. DV 21-25; PONTIFICAL BIBLICAL COMMISSION, *The interpretation of the Bible in the Church* (21 September 1993), especially in IV, see 2 and 3, Città del Vaticano 1993.

[34] SRS 41; cf. CA 5, 53-62. CONGREGATION FOR CATHOLIC EDUCATION, *Guidelines for the study and teaching of the Social Doctrine of the Church in the formation of priests* (30 December, 1988), Rome 1988.

and silence. It must be regarded as an "eminent kind of catechesis".[35]

 – Occasional catechesis which seeks to interpret determined circumstances of personal, family, ecclesial or social life and to help live them in the prospect offaith.[36]

 – Initiatives of spiritual formation which seek to reinforce conviction, open new prospectives and encourage perseverance in prayer and in the duties of following Christ.

 – A systematic deepening of the Christian message by means of theological instruction, so as truly to educate in the faith, encourage growth in understanding of it and to equip the Christian for giving the reason for his hope in the present world.[37] In a certain sense, it is appropriate to call such instruction "perfective catechesis".

72.   It is fundamentally important that initiatory catechesis for adults, whether baptized or not, initiatory catechesis for children and young people and continuing catechesis are closely linked with the catechetical endeavour of the Christian community, so that the particular Church may grow harmoniously and that its evangelizing activity may spring from authentic sources. "It is important also that the catechesis of children and young people, permanent catechesis and the catechesis of adults should not be separate watertight compartments... it is important that their perfect complementarity be fostered".[38]

[35] CT 23. Cf. SC 35 ad 3; CIC 777, 1 and 2.
[36] Cf. CT 21c and 47; DCG (1971) 96 c, d, e, f.
[37] Cf. 1 Pt 3,15 CONGREGATION FOR THE DOCTRINE OF THE FAITH, Instruction *Dominum veritatis,* n. 6b *l.c.* 1552. Confer also what is indicated in CT 61, about the correlation between catechesis and theology.
[38] CT 45c.

CATECHESIS AND RELIGIOUS INSTRUCTION IN SCHOOLS

The proper character of religious instruction in schools

73. Within the ministry of the word, the character proper to religious instruction in schools and its relationship with the catechesis of children and of young people merit special consideration.

The relationship between religious instruction in schools and catechesis is one of distinction and complementarity: "there is an absolute necessity to distinguish clearly between religious instruction and catechesis".[39]

What confers on religious instruction in schools its proper evangelizing character is the fact that it is called to penetrate a particular area of culture and to relate with other areas of knowledge. As an original form of the ministry of the word, it makes present the Gospel in a personal process of cultural, systematic and critical assimilation.[40]

In the cultural universe, which is assimilated by students and which is defined by knowledge and values offered by other scholastic disciplines, religious instruction in schools sows the dynamic seed of the Gospel and seeks to "keep in touch with the other elements of the student's knowledge and education; thus the Gospel will impregnate the mentality of the students in the field of their learning, and the harmonization of their culture will be achieved in the light of faith".[41]

---

[39] CONGREGATION FOR CATHOLIC EDUCATION, "The religious dimension of education in the catholic school" (7 April 1988), n. 68; Tipografia Poliglotta Vaticana, Roma 1988 cf. JOHN PAUL II, *Allocution* to the priests of the diocese of Rome (5 March 1981). *Insegnamenti di Giovanni Paolo II*, IV 1 pp. 629-630, CD 13c CIC 761.

[40] SACRED CONGREGATION FOR CATHOLIC EDUCATION, Document, *The Catholic school* (19 March 1977) n. 26, Typographie Polyglotte Vaticane 1977.

[41] CT 69. Note also as per CT 69 the originality of religious instruction in schools does not consist solely in rendering possible dialogue with culture in general since this pertains to all the forms of ministry of the word. Religious instruction in

It is necessary, therefore, that religious instruction in schools appear as a scholastic discipline with the same systematic demands and the same rigour as other disciplines. It must present the Christian message and the Christian event with the same seriousness and the same depth with which other disciplines present their knowledge. It should not be an accessory alongside of these disciplines, but rather it should engage in a necessary interdisciplinary dialogue. This dialogue should take place above all at that level at which every discipline forms the personality of students. In this way the presentation of the Christian message influences the way in which the origins of the world, the sense of history, the basis of ethical values, the function of religion in culture, the destiny of man and his relationship with nature, are understood. Through inter-disciplinary dialogue religious instruction in schools underpins, activates, develops and completes the educational activity of the school.[42]

The school context and those to whom religious instruction in schools is directed

74. Religious instruction in schools is developed in diverse scholastic contexts, while always maintaining its proper character, to acquire different emphases. These depend on legal and organizational circumstances, educational theories, personal outlook of individual teachers and students as well as the relationship between religious instruction in the schools and family or parish catechesis.

---

schools seeks in a more immediate way to promote this dialogue in a personal process of systematic and critical initiation and by encounter with the cultural patrimony promoted by the school.

[42] Cf. CONGREGATION FOR CATHOLIC EDUCATION, *"The religious dimension of education in the Catholic school"*, l.c. 70.

It is not possible to reduce the various forms of religious instruction in schools, which have developed as a result of accords between individual states and Episcopal Conferences. It is, however, necessary that efforts be made so that religious instruction in schools respond to its objectives and its own characteristics.[43]

Students "have the right to learn with truth and certainty the religion to which they belong. This right to know Christ, and the salvific message proclaimed by Him cannot be neglected. The confessional character of religious instruction in schools, in its various focuses, given by the Church in different countries is an indispensible guarantee offered to families and students who choose such education".[44]

When given in the context of the Catholic school, religious instruction is part of and completed by other forms of the ministry of the word (catechesis, homilies, liturgical celebration, etc.). It is indispinsible to their pedagogical function and the basis for their existence.[45]

In the context of state schools or non-confessional schools where the civil authorities or other circumstances impose the teaching of religion common to both Catholics and non Catholics[46] it will have a more ecumenical character and have a more inter-religious awareness.

In other circumstances religious instruction will have an extensively cultural character and teach a knowledge of religions including the Catholic religion. In this case too and expecially if presented by teachers with a sincere respect for the Christian re-

[43] Cf. JOHN PAUL II, *Allocution* on the Symposium of the Council of the Episcopal Conference on the the Teaching of the Catholic Religion in the public school (15 April 1991): *Teachings of John Paul II,* XIV/1, pp. 780s.

[44] *Ibid.*

[45] Cf. CT 69, CONGREGATION FOR CATHOLIC EDUCATION, *The religious dimension of education in the Catholic school,* n. 66: l.c.

[46] Cf. CT 33.

ligion, religious instruction maintains a true dimension of "evangelic preparation".[47]

75.   The life and faith of students who receive religious instruction in school are characterized by continuous change. Religious instruction should be cognizant of that fact if it is to accomplish its own ends. In the case of students who are believers, religious instruction assists them to understand better the Christian message, by relating it to the great existential concerns common to all religions and to every human being, to the various visions of life particularly evident in culture and to those major moral questions which confront humanity today.

Those students who are searching, or who have religious doubts, can also find in religious instruction the possibility of discovering what exactly faith in Jesus Christ is, what response the Church makes to their questions, and gives them the opportunity to examine their own choice more deeply.

In the case of students who are non-believers, religious instruction assumes the character of a missionary proclamation of the Gospel and is ordered to a decision of faith, which catechesis, in its turn, will nurture and mature.

Education in the Christian family, catechesis and religious instruction at the service of education in the faith

76.   Christian education in the family, catechesis and religious instruction in schools are, each in its own way, closely interrelated with the service of Christian education of children, adolescents, and young people. In practice, however, different factors must be taken into consideration in order to proceed realistically and with pastoral prudence in the application of general guidelines.

[47] Cf. CT 34.

It is for each diocese or pastoral region to discern the diverse circumstances which arise with regard to the existence or not of Christian initiation of children in the context of the family, and with regard to the formative duties which are traditionally exercised by the parish, the school etc. Consequently the particular Church and the Episcopal Conference shall establish proper guidelines for various situations and foster distinct but complementary activities.

CHAPTER III

The nature, object and the duties of catechesis

"And every tongue confess that Jesus Christ is Lord, to the glory of God the Father (Phil 2:11).

---

77. Having outlined the place of catechesis in the Church's mission of evangelization, its relationship with the various elements of evangelization, and with other forms of the ministry of the word, this chapter examines catechesis particularly in relation to:

– the ecclesial nature of catechesis, that is to say, the agent of catechesis, the Church animated by the Holy Spirit;

– the fundamental object of catechesis;

– the tasks whereby this objective is achieved and which constitute its more immediate objectives;

– the gradual nature of the catechetical process and its catechumenal inspiration.

Moreover, in this chapter, the proper character of catechesis—already described in the preceding chapter—is examined through the analysis of its relationship with other ecclesial activities.

Catechesis: activity of an ecclesial nature

78.   Catechesis is an essentially ecclesial act. [1] The true subject of catechesis is the Church which, continuing the mission of Jesus the Master and, therefore animated by the Holy Spirit, is sent to be the teacher of the faith. The Church imitates the Mother of the Lord in treasuring the Gospel in her heart.[2] She proclaims it, celebrates it, lives it, and she transmits it in catechesis to all those who have decided to follow Jesus Christ. This transmission of the Gospel is a living act of ecclesial tradition: [3]

– The Church transmits the faith which she herself lives: her understanding of the mystery of God and his salvific plan, her vision of man's highest vocation, the style of evangelic life which communicates the joy of the Kingdom, the hope which pervades her and the love which she has for mankind and all God's creatures.

– The Church transmits the faith in an active way; she sows it in the hearts of catechumens and those to be catechized so as to nourish their profoundest experience of life.[4] The profession of faith received by the Church (*traditio*), which germinates and grows during the catechetical process, is given back (*redditio*), enriched by the values of different cultures. [5] The catechumenate is

---

[1] As has been stated in chapter I of this part in "The transmission of Revelation by the Church, the work of the Holy Spirit" and in part II, chapter I in "The ecclesial nature of the Gospel message". Cf. EN 60 which speaks of the ecclesial nature of any evangelizing activity.

[2] Cf. LG 64; DV 10a.

[3] Cf. DCG (1971) 13.

[4] Cf. AG 22a.

[5] Cf. CT 28, RCIA 25 and 183-187. The *traditio-redditio symboli* (the handing over and giving back of the Creed) is an important element of the baptismal catechumenate. The bipolarity of this gesture expresses the double dimension of the faith: the received gift (*traditio*) and the personal and enculturated response (*redditio*). Cf. CT 28 for Aan adequate use in catechesis of this most expressive rite.

thus transformed into a centre of deepening catholicity and a ferment of ecclesial renewal.

79.   In transmitting faith and new life, the Church acts as a mother for mankind who begets children conceived by the power of the Spirit and born of God.[6] Precisely "because she is a mother, she is also the educator of our faith"; [7] she is at the same time mother and teacher. Through catechesis she feeds her children with her own faith and incorporates them as members into the ecclesial family. As a good mother she gives them the Gospel in all its authenticity and purity as apposite food, culturally enriched and a response to the deepest aspirations of the human heart.

The object of catechesis: communion with Jesus Christ

80.   "The definitive aim of catechesis is to put people not only in touch, but also in communion and intimacy, with Jesus Christ". [8] All evangelizing activity is understood as promoting communion with Jesus Christ. Starting with the "initial" [9] conversion of a person to the Lord, moved by the Holy Spirit through the primary proclamation of the Gospel, catechesis seeks to solidify and mature this first adherence. It proposes to help those who have just converted "to know better this Jesus to whom he has entrusted himself: to know his 'mystery', the king-

---

[6] Cf. LG 64.

[7] CCC 169. The relation between the *maternity of the Church* and her *educative function* is expressed very well by St Gregory the Great: *"Having been made fruitful by conceiving her children thanks to the ministry of preaching, causes them to grow in her womb by her teaching. Moralia* XIX, c. 12, 9; PL 76, 108).

[8] CT 5; cf. CCC 426; AG 14a. In relation to this christological end of catechesis see Part I, chap. I and Part II, chap. I. *"Jesus Christ mediator and fullness of Revelation"* and that which is said in II part, chapter 1 *"Christiaity of the evagelical mission"*.

[9] AG 13b.

dom of God proclaimed by him, the requirements and comments contained in his Gospel message, and the paths that he has laid down for anyone who wishes to follow him".[10] Baptism, the sacrament by which "we are configured to Christ",[11] sustains this work of catechesis with the help of its grace.

81. Communion with Jesus Christ, by its own dynamic, leads the disciple to unite himself with everything with which Jesus Christ himself was profoundly united: with God his Father, who sent him into the world, and with the Holy Spirit, who impelled his mission; with the Church, his body, for which he gave himself up, with mankind and with his brothers whose lot he wished to share.

The object of catechesis is expressed in profession of faith in the one God: Father, Son and Holy Spirit

82. Catechesis is that particular form of the ministry of the word which matures initial conversion to make it into a living, explicit and fruitful confession of faith: *"Catechesis has its origin in the confession of faith and leads to confession of faith."*[12]

The profession of faith inherent in Baptism [13] is eminently Trinitarian. The Church baptizes *"in the name of the Father and of the Son and of the Holy Spirit"* (*Mt* 28,19) [14] the triune God to whom the Christian entrusts his life. Initiatory catechesis—both before and after the reception of Baptism—prepares for this decisive undertaking. Continuing catechesis helps to mature this profession of faith, to proclaim it in the Eucharist and to renew

---

[10] CT 20c.
[11] LG 7b.
[12] MPD 8; CCC 185-197.
[13] Cf. CCC 189.
[14] Cf. CCC 180-190 and 197.

the commitments which it entails. It is important that catechesis should unite well the confession of christological faith, *"Jesus is Lord"*, with the trinitarian confession, *"I believe in the Father, the Son and the Holy Spirit"*, in such a way that there are not two modes of expressing the Christian faith. He who is converted to Jesus Christ and recognizes him as Lord through the primary proclamation of the Gospel begins a process which, aided by catechesis, necessarily leads to explicit confession of the Trinity.

In the confession of faith in the one God, the Christian rejects all service of any human absolute; "power, pleasure, race, ancestors, state, wealth...",[15] and is thus liberated from the enslavement of any idol. It is the proclamation of his will to serve God and man without any ties. In proclaiming faith in the Trinity, which is a communion of Persons, the disciple of Jesus Christ shows at once that the love of God and neighbour is the principle which informs his being and his action.

83. The confession of faith is complete only in reference to the Church. All the baptized individually proclaim the *Credo,* for no action can be more personal than this. However, they recite it in the Church and through the Church, because they do so as members of the Church. 'Credo' and 'Credimus' necessarily imply each other.[16] In fusing his confession of faith with that of the Church, the Christian is incorporated into her mission: to be the "universal sacrament of salvation" for the life of the world. He who makes the profession of faith takes on responsibilities that not infrequently provoke persecution. In Christian history the martyrs are proclaimers and witnesses par excellence.[17]

---

[15] Cf. CCC 2113.
[16] Cf. CCC 166-67; CCC 196.
[17] Cf. RM 45.

The tasks of catechesis accomplish its objective

84. The object of catechesis is realized by diverse, interrelated tasks.[18] To carry them out, catechesis is certainly inspired by the manner in which Jesus formed his disciples. He made known to them the different dimensions of the Kingdom of God: "to you it has been given to know the secrets of the Kingdom of heaven" (*Mt* 13,11).[19] He taught them to pray (*"When you pray, say Father... Lk* 11,2).[20] He impressed upon them evangelic attitudes (*"learn from me for I am gentle and lowly in heart" Mt* 11,29) He prepared them for mission (*"He sent them on ahead of him two by two..." Lk* 10,1)[21]

The duties of catechesis correspond to education of the different dimensions of faith, for catechesis is integral Christian formation, *"open to all the other factors of Christian life"*.[22] In virtue of its own internal dynamic, the faith demands to be known, celebrated, lived and translated into prayer. Catechesis must cultivate each of these dimensions. The faith, however, is lived out by the Christian community and proclaimed in mission: it is a shared and proclaimed faith. These dimensions must also be encouraged by catechesis. The Second Vatican Council expresses these duties as follows: "...catechetical instruction, which illumines and strengthens the faith develops a life in harmony with the Spirit of Christ, stimulates a conscious and fervent participa-

---

[18] The DCG (1971) 21-29 also distinguishes between the end (*finis*) and the means (*munera*) of catechesis. These are the specific objectives in which the end is concretized.

[19] Cf. *Mk* 4:10-12.

[20] Cf. *Mt* 6: 5-6.

[21] Cf. *Mt* 10,5-15.

[22] CT 21b.

tion in the liturgical mystery and encourages men to take an active part in the apostolate".[23]

Fundamental tasks of catechesis: helping to know, to celebrate and to contemplate the mystery of Christ

85. The fundamental tasks of catechesis are:

– *Promoting knowledge of the faith*

Who has encountered Christ desires to know him as much as possible, as well as to know the plan of the Father which he revealed. Knowledge of the faith (*fides quae*) is required by adherence to the faith (*fides qua*).[24] Even in the human order the love which one person has for another causes that person to wish to know the other all the more. Catechesis, must, therefore, lead to "the gradual grasping of the whole truth about the divine plan",[25] by introducing the disciples of Jesus to a knowledge of Tradition and of Scripture, which is "*thesublime science of Christ*".[26] By deepening knowledge of the faith, catechesis nourishes not only the life of faith but equips it to explain itself to the world. The meaning of the Creed, which is a compendium of Scripture and of the faith of the Church, is the realization of this task.

– *Liturgical education*

Christ is always present in his Church, especially in "liturgical celebrations".[27] Communion with Jesus Christ leads to the celebration of his salvific presence in the sacraments, especially in the Eucharist. The Church ardently desires that all the Christian

---

[23] GE 4; cf. RICA 19, CIC 788,2.
[24] Cf. DCG (1971) 36a.
[25] Cf. DCG (1971) 24.
[26] DV 25a.
[27] SC 7.

faithful be brought to that full, conscious and active participation which is required by the very nature of the liturgy [28] and the dignity of the baptismal priesthood. For this reason, catechesis, along with promoting a knowledge of the meaning of the liturgy and the sacraments, must also educate the disciples of Jesus Christ "for prayer, for thanksgiving, for repentance, for praying with confidence, for community spirit, for understanding correctly the meaning of the creeds...",[29] as all of this is necessary for a true liturgical life

– Moral formation

Conversion to Jesus Christ implies walking in his footsteps. Catechesis must, therefore, transmit to the disciples the attitudes of the Master himself. The disciples thus undertake a journey of interior transformation, in which, by participating in the paschal mystery of the Lord, "they pass from the old man to the new man who has been made perfect in Christ".[30] The Sermon on the Mount, in which Jesus takes up the Decalogue, and impresses upon it the spirit of the beatitudes,[31] is an indispensable point of reference for the moral formation which is most necessary today. Evangelization which "involves the proclamation and presentation of morality",[32] displays all the force of its appeal where it offers not only the proclaimed word but the lived word too. This moral testimony, which is prepared for by catechesis, must always demonstrate the social consequences of the demands of the Gospel.[33]

[28] Cf. SC 14.
[29] DCG (1971) 25b.
[30] AG 13.
[31] Cf. LG 62; CCC 1965-1986. The CCC 1697 specifies in particular the characteristics which catechesis must assume in moral formation.
[32] VS 107.
[33] Cf. CT 29f.

– Teaching to pray

Communion with Jesus Christ leads the disciples to assume the attitude of prayer and contemplation which the Master himself had. To learn to pray with Jesus is to pray with the same sentiments with which he turned to the Father: adoration, praise, thanksgiving, filial confidence, supplication and awe for his glory. All of these sentiments are reflected in the *Our Father*, the prayer which Jesus taught his disciples and which is the model of all Christian prayer. The *"handing on of the Our Father"* [34] is a summary of the entire Gospel [35] and is therefore a true act of catechesis. When catechesis is permeated by a climate of prayer, the assimilation of the entire Christian life reaches its summit. This climate is especially necessary when the catechumen and those to be catechized are confronted with the more demanding aspects of the Gospel and when they feel weak or when they discover the mysterious action of God in their lives.

Other fundamental tasks of catechesis: initiation and education in community life and to mission

86.   Catechesis prepares the Christian to live in community and to participate actively in the life and mission of the Church. The Second Vatican Council indicates the necessity for pastors "to form genuine Christian communities" [36] and for catechumens "[to] learn to co-operate actively in building up the Church and its work of evangelization". [37]

---

[34] RCIA 25 and 188-191.
[35] Cf. CCC 2761.
[36] PO 6d.
[37] AG 14d.

– Education for Community Life

a) Christian community life is not realized spontaneously. It is necessary to educate it carefully. In this apprenticeship, the teaching of Christ on community life, recounted in the Gospel of St Matthew, calls for attitudes which it is for catechesis to inculcate: the spirit of simplicity and humility (*"unless you turn and become like little children..." Mt* 18,3); solicitude for the least among the brethren (*"but whoever causes one of these little ones who believe in me to sin..." Mt* 18,6); particular care for those who are alienated (*"Go and search of the one that went astray..." Mt* 18,12); fraternal correction (*"Go and tell him his fault..." Mt* 18,15); common prayer (*"if two of you agree on earth to ask about anything..." Mt* 18,19); mutual forgiveness (*"but seventy times seven..." Mt* 18,22). Fraternal love embraces all these attitudes (*"love one another; even as I have loved you..." Jn* 13,34).

b) In developing this community sense, catechesis takes special note of the ecumenical dimension and encourages fraternal attitudes toward members of other Christian churches and ecclesial communities. Thus catechesis in pursuing this objective should give a clear exposition of all the Church's doctrine and avoid formulations or expressions that might give rise to error. It also implies "a suitable knowledge of other confessions",[38] with which there are shared elements of faith: "the written word of God, the life of grace, faith, hope and charity, and the other interior gifts of the Holy Spirit".[39] Catechesis will possess an ecumenical dimension in the measure in which it arouses and nourishes "a true desire for unity",[40] not easy irenicism, but perfect unity, when the Lord himself wills it and by those means by which he wishes that it should be brought about.

---

[38] DCG (1971) 27.
[39] UR 3b.
[40] CT 32; cf. CCC 821; CT 34.

– *Missionary initiation*

a) Catechesis is also open to the missionary dimension.[41] This seeks to equip the disciples of Jesus to be present as Christians in society through their professional, cultural and social lives. It also prepares them to lend their cooperation to the different ec- clesial services, according to their proper vocation. This task of evangelization originates, for the lay faithful, in the sacraments of Christian initiation and in the secular character of their voca- tion.[42] It is also important that every means should be used to encourage vocations to the Priesthood, and to the different forms of consecration to God in religious and apostolic life and to awaken special missionary vocations. The evangelical attitudes which Jesus taught his disciples when he sent them on mission are precisely those which catechesis must nourish: to seek out the lost sheep, proclaim and heal at the same time, to be poor, without money or knapsack; to know how to accept rejection and persecution; to place one's trust in the Father and in the support of the Holy Spirit; to expect no other reward than the joy of working for the Kingdom.[43]

b) In educating for this missionary sense, catechesis is also necessary for interreligious dialogue, if it renders the faithful ca- pable of meaningful communication with men and women of other religions.[44] Catechesis shows that the link between the Church and non-Christian religions is, in the first place, the com- mon origin and end of the human race, as well as the "many seeds of the word which God has sown in these religions". Cat- echesis too helps to reconcile and, at the same time, to distin- guish between "the proclamation of Christ" and "inter-religious

---

[41] Cf. CT 24b and DCG (1971) 28.
[42] Cf. LG 31b and ChL 15; CCC 898-900.
[43] Cf. *Mt* 10:5-42 and *Lk* 10:1-20.
[44] Cf. EN 53 and RM 55-57.

dialogue". These two elements, while closely connected, must not be confused or identified.[45] Indeed, "dialogue does not dispencse form evangelization".[46]

Observations on the totality of these tasks

87. The tasks of catechesis, consequently, constitute a totality, rich and varied in aspect. On this point it is opportune to make some observations.

– "All of these tasks are necessary. As the vitality of the human body depends on the proper function of all of its organs, so also the maturation of the Christian life requires that it be cultivated in all its dimensions: knowledge of the faith, liturgical life, moral formation, prayer, belonging to community, missionary spirit. When catechesis omits one of these elements, the Christian faith does not attain full development.

– Each task realizes, in its own way, the object of catechesis. Moral formation, for example, is essentially christological and trinitarian. It is deeply ecclesial, while also open to social concerns. The same is true of liturgical formation. While essentially religious and ecclesial, it also strongly demands commitment to the evangelization of the world.

– These tasks are interdependent and develop together. Each great catechetical theme—catechesis of God the Father, for example—has a cognitive dimension as well as moral implications. It is interiorized in prayer and appropriated in witness. One task

---

[45] Cf. RM 55b; CONGREGATION FOR THE EVANGELIZATION OF PEOPLES AND THE PONTIFICAL COUNCIL FOR INTER-RELIGIOUS DIALOGUE, *"Dialogue and Proclamation"* (19 may 1991), nn. 14-54; AAS 84 (1992), pp. 419-432. CCC 839-845; Part IV, chap. 4 of this Directory refers to those to whom catechesis is addressed and returns to the topic *Catechesis in the context of other religions.*

[46] RM 55a.

echoes the other: knowledge of the faith prepares for mission; the sacramental life gives strength for moral transformation.

– To fulfil its tasks, catechesis avails of two principal means: transmission of the Gospel message and experience of the Christian life.[47] Liturgical formation, for example, must explain what the Christian liturgy is, and what the sacraments are. It must also however, offer an experience of the different kinds of celebration and it must make symbols, gestures, etc. known and loved. Moral formation not only transmits the content of Christian morality, but also cultivates active evangelical attitudes and Christian values.

– The different dimensions of faith are objects of formation, as much of being given as received. Knowledge of the faith, liturgical life, the following of Christ are all a gift of the Spirit which are received in prayer, and similarly a duty of spiritual and moral study and witness. Neither aspect may be neglected.[48]

– Every dimension of the faith, like the faith itself as a whole, must be rooted in human experience and not remain a mere adjunct to the human person. Knowledge of the faith is significant. It gives light to the whole of existence and dialogues with culture. In the liturgy, all personal life becomes a spiritual oblation. The morality of the Gospel assumes and elevates human values. Prayer is open to all personal and social problems.[49]

As the 1971 Directory indicates, "it is very important that catechesis retain the richness of these various aspects in such a way that one aspect is not separated from the rest to the detriment of the others".[50]

---

[47] Cf. CIC 773 and 778 § 2.
[48] Cf. DCG (1971) 22 and 23.
[49] Cf. DCG (1971) 26.
[50] DCG (1971) 31b.

The baptismal catechumenate: structure and progression

88.   Faith, moved by divine grace and cultivated by the action of the Church, undergoes a process of maturation. Catechesis, which is at the service of this growth, is also a gradual activity. "Good catechesis is always done in steps".[51] In the baptismal catechumenate, formation is articulated in four stages:

– *the pre-catechumenate,*[52] characterized as the locus of first evangelization leading to conversion and where the kerygma of the primary proclamation is explained;

– *the catechumenate,*[53] properly speaking, the context of integral catechesis beginning with "the handing on of the Gospels"; [54]

– a time of *purification and illumination*[55] which affords a more intense preparation for the sacraments of initiation and in which the "the handing on of the Creed"[56] and "the handing on of the Lord's Prayer" take place; [57]

– a time of *mystagogy,*[58] characterized by the experience of the sacraments and entry into the community.

89.   These stages, which reflect the wisdom of the great catechumenal tradition, also inspire the gradual nature of catechesis.[59]

---

[51] Cf. RCIA 19.

[52] RCIA 9-13.

[53] RCIA 14-20; 68-72; 98-105.

[54] RCIA 93; cf. MPD 8c.

[55] RCIA 21-26; 133-142; 152-159.

[56] RCIA 25 and 183-187.

[57] RCIA 25 and 188-192.

[58] RCIA 37-40; 35-239.

[59] This gradual nature is also apparent in the names which the Church uses to designate those who are in the various stages of the baptismal catechumenate: *sympathizers* (RCIA 12), those who are disposed to the faith but do not yet fully believe; *catechumens* (RCIA 17-18), those who have firmly decided to follow Jesus; *elect* (RCIA 24), those called to receive Baptism; *neophytes* (RCIA 31-36) those just born

In the patristic period properly, catechumenal formation was realized through biblical catechesis, based on recounting the history of salvation; immediate preparation for Baptism by doctrinal catechesis, explaining the Creed and the *Our Father* which had just been handed on, together with their moral implications; and through the phase following the sacraments of initiation, a period of mystagogical catechesis which help the newly baptized to interiorize these sacraments and incorporate themselves into the community. This patristic concept continues to illuminate the present catechumenate and initiatory catechesis itself. This latter, in so far as it accompanies the process of conversion, is essentially gradual and, in so far as it is at the service of one who has decided to follow Christ, it is eminently christocentric.

The baptismal catechumenate: inspiration for catechesis in the Church

90.   Given that the *missio ad gentes* is the paradigm of all the Church's missionary activity, the baptismal catechumenate, which is joined to it, is the model of its catechizing activity.[60] It is therefore helpful to underline those elements of the catechumenate which must inspire contemporary catechesis and its significance.

By way of premise, however, it must be said that there is a fundamental difference between catechumens those being catechized,[61] between the *pre-baptismal* catechesis and the *post-baptismal* catechesis, which is respectively imparted to them. The latter derives from the sacraments of initiation which were received

into the light by the grace of Baptism; *the Christian faithful* (RCIA 39), those who are mature in the faith and active members of the Christian community.

[60]   Cf. MPD 8; EN 44; ChL 61.

[61]   In this DCG the expressions 'catechumens' and 'those being catechized' are used to make this distinction. For its part the CIC, canons 204-206, notes the different ways by which catechumens and the Christian faithful have union with the Church.

as infants, "who have been already introduced into the Church and have been made sons of God by means of Baptism. The basis of their conversion is the Baptism which they have already received and whose power they must develop".[62]

91. In view of this substantial difference, some elements of the baptismal catechumenate are now considered, as the source of inspiration for post-baptismal catechesis.

– the baptismal catechumenate constantly reminds the whole Church of the fundamental importance of the function of initiation and the basic factors which constitute it: catechesis and the sacraments of Baptism, Confirmation and Eucharist. The pastoral care of Christian initiation is vital for every particular Church.

– The baptismal catechumenate is the responsibility of the entire Christian community. Indeed "this Christian initiation which takes place during the catechumenate should not be left entirely to the priests and catechists, but should be the care of the entire Christian community, especially the sponsors".[63] The institution of the catechumenate thus increases awareness of the spiritual maternity of the Church, which she exercises in every form of education in the faith.[64]

– The baptismal catechumenate is also completely permeated by the *mystery of Christ's Passover*. For this reason, "all initiation

---

[62] RCIA 295. The same *Rite of Christian Initiation of Adults*, chap. 4, ponders the question of those baptized adults who need initiatory catechesis. CT 44 specifies the diverse circumstances in which this catechesis may be deemed necessary.

[63] AG 14d.

[64] Methodius of Olympus, for example, speaks of this *maternal action* of the Christian community when he says: With regard to those who are still imperfect (in the Christian life), it is for the more mature to form them and to bring them to birth as a mother. (*Symposium*, III, 8; GCS 27, 88). See also St Gregory the Great *Homilia in Evangelia*, I, III, 2; PL 76,1086 D).

must reveal clearly its paschal nature.[65] The Easter Vigil, focal point of the Christian liturgy, and its spirituality of Baptism inspire all catechesis.

– The baptismal catechumenate is also an initial locus of inculturation. Following the example of the Incarnation of the Son of God, made man in a concrete historical moment, the Church receives catechumens integrally, together with their cultural ties. All catechetical activity participates in this function of incorporating into the catholicity of the Church, authentic "seeds of the word", scattered through nations and individuals.[66]

– Finally, the concept of the baptismal catechumenate as *a process of formation and as a true school of the faith* offers post-baptismal catechesis dynamic and particular characteristics: comprehensiveness and integrity of formation; its gradual character expressed in definite stages; its connection with meaningful rites, symbols, biblical and liturgical signs; its constant references to the Christian community.

Post-baptismal catechesis, without slavishly imitating the structure of the baptismal catechumenate, and recognizing in those to be catechized the reality of their Baptism, does well, however, to draw inspiration from "this preparatory school for the Christian life",[67] and to allow itself to be enriched by those principal elements which characterize the catechumenate.

---

[65] RCIA 8.

[66] Cf. CT 53.

[67] DCG (1971) 130. This article begins with the affirmation: "The catechumenate for adults, which at one and the same time includes catechesis, liturgical participation and community living, is an excellent example of an institute that springs from the cooperation of diverse pastoral functions".

PART II

THE GOSPEL MESSAGE

The Gospel Message

"And this is eternal life, that they know thee the only true God, and Jesus Christ whom thou has sent" (Jn 17:3).

"Jesus came into Galilee, preaching the Gospel of God, and saying, 'The time is fulfilled, and the kingdom of God is at hand; repent and believe in the Gospel'" (Mk 1:14-15).

"Now I would remind you, brethren, in what terms I preached to you the Gospel, which you received, in which you stand, by which you are saved, if you hold it fast—unless you believed in vain. For I delivered to you as of first importance what I also received, that Christ died for our sins in accordance with the Scriptures, that he was buried, that he was raised on the third day to life in accordance with the Scriptures" (1 Cor 15:1-4).

The meaning and purpose of Part Two

92. The Christian faith, through which a person says "Yes" to Jesus Christ, may be analysed thus:

– as an adherence, which is given under the influence of grace, to God who reveals himself; in this case the faith consists in believing the word of God and committing oneself to it (*fides qua*);

– as the content of Revelation and of the Gospel message; in this sense, faith is expressed in its endeavour to understand better the mystery of the word (*fides quae*).

Both aspects, by their very nature, cannot be separated. Maturation and growth in the faith require their comprehensive and coherent development. For methodological purposes, however, they can be regarded separately.[1]

93. *Part Two*, considers the content of the Gospel message (*fides quae*).

— The first chapter, sets out the norms and criteria which catechesis must follow so as to find, formulate and present its contents. Indeed every form of the ministry of the word is ordered to the presentation of the Gospel message according to its own character.

— The second chapter examines the content of the faith as it is presented in the *Catechism of the Catholic Church*, which is the doctrinal point of reference for all catechesis. It also presents some observations which may help the assimilation and interiorization of the Catechism and locate it within the catechetical activity of the Church. In addition, some criteria are set out to assist particular Churches in compiling catechisms based on the *Catechism of the Catholic Church*, which, while preserving the unity of the faith, must also take into account diversity of circumstances and cultures.

[1] Cf. DCG (1971) 36a.

CHAPTER I

Norms and criteria for presenting the Gospel message in catechesis

"Hear, O Israel: The Lord our God is one Lord; and you shall love the Lord your God with all your heart, and with all your soul, and with all your might. And these words which I command you this day shall be upon your heart; and you shall teach them diligently to your children, and shall talk of them when you sit in your house, and when you walk by the way, and when you lie down, and when you rise. And you shall bind them as a sign upon your hand, and they shall be as frontlets between your eyes. And you shall write them on the doorposts of your house and on your gates" (Dt 6:4-9).

"And the Word became flesh and dwelt among us" (Jn 1:14).

The word of God: source of catechesis

94.   The source from which catechesis draws its message is the word of God:

> "Catechesis will always draw its content from the living source of the word of God transmitted in Tradition and the Scriptures, for sacred Tradition and sacred Scripture make up a single sacred deposit of the word of God, which is entrusted to the Church".[1]

This "deposit of faith" [2] is like the treasure of a householder; it is entrusted to the Church, the family of God, and she

---

[1] CT 27.
[2] Cf. DV 10 a e b; cf. 1 Tim 6:20 and 2 Tim 1:14.

continuously draws from it things new and old.[3] All God's children, animated by his Spirit, are nourished by this treasure of the Word. They know that the Word is Jesus Christ, the Word made man and that his voice continues to resound in the Church and in the world through the Holy Spirit. The Word of God, by wondrous divine "condescension"[4] is directed toward us and reaches us by means of human "deeds and words", "just as the Word of the eternal Father, when he took on himself the flesh of human weakness, became like men".[5] And so without ceasing to be the word of God, it is expressed in human words. Although close to us, it still remains veiled, in a "kenotic" state. Thus the Church, guided by the Holy Spirit, has to interpret the word continually. She contemplates the word with a profound spirit of faith, "listens to [it] devotedly, guards it with dedication and expounds it faithfully".[6]

The source and the "sources" of the message of catechesis [7]

95. The *word of God,* contained in Sacred Tradition and in Sacred Scripture:

– is mediated upon and understood more deeply by means of the sense of faith of all the people of God, guided by the Magisterium which teaches with authority;

---

[3] Cf. *Mt* 13:52.
[4] DV 13.
[5] *Ibid.*
[6] DV 10.
[7] As can be seen both expressions, the source and the *sourcees,* are used. The term 'the source of catechesis' is used to underline the oneness of the word of God and recalls the concept of Revelation in *Dei Verbum.* CT 27 also speaks of 'the source' of catechesis. Nonetheless following general catechetical usage the expression 'the sources' is used to denote those concrete loci from which catechesis draws its message; cf. DCG (1971) 45.

– is celebrated in the Sacred Liturgy, where it is constantly proclaimed, heard, interiorized and explained;

– shines forth in the life of the Church, in her two-thousand-year history, especially in Christian witness and particularly in that of the saints;

– is deepened by theological research which helps believers to advance in their vital understanding of the mysteries of faith;

– is made manifest in genuine religious and moral values which, as "seeds of the word", are sown in human society and diverse cultures.

96.   These are all the sources, principle or subsidiary, of catechesis but must not be understood in a narrow sense.[8] Sacred Scripture "is the speech of God as it is put down in writing under the breath of the Holy Spirit",[9] Sacred Tradition "transmits in its entirety the word of God which has been entrusted to the apostles by Christ the Lord and the Holy Spirit".[10] The Magisterium has the duty of "giving an authentic interpretation of the word of God",[11] and in doing so fulfils, in the name of Christ, a fundamental ecclesial service. Tradition, Scripture and the Magisterium, all three of which are closely connected, are "each according to its own way",[12] the principle sources of catechesis. Each of the subsidiary sources of catechesis has its own proper language which has been shaped by a rich variety of "documents of the faith". Catechesis is a living tradition of such documents: [13] biblical excerpts, liturgical texts, patristic writings, for-

---

[8] Cf. DCG (1971) 45b.
[9] DV 9.
[10] *Ibid.*
[11] DV 10b.
[12] DV 10c.
[13] Cf. MPD 9.

mulations of the Magisterium, creeds, testimonies of the saints and theological reflections.

The living source of the word of God and the "sources" deriving from it, and through which it is expressed, provide catechesis with those criteria for the transmission of its message to all who have made their decision to follow Jesus Christ.

Criteria for the presentation of the message

97.   The criteria for presenting the Gospel message in catechesis are closely inter-connected with each other as they spring from the same source.

– The message centred on the person of Jesus Christ (*christocentricity*), by its inherent dynamic, introduces the trinitarian dimension of the same message.

– The proclamation of the Good News of the Kingdom of God, centred on the *gift of Salvation*, implies a message of *liberation*.

– The *ecclesial* character of the message reflects its *historic* nature because catechesis—as with all evangelization—is realized within "the time of the Church".

– The Gospel message seeks *inculturation* because the Good News is destined for all peoples. This can only be accomplished when the Gospel message is presented in its *integrity and purity*.

– The Gospel message is a *comprehensive message,* with its own hierarchy of truth. It is this harmonious vision of the Gospel which converts it into a profoundly *meaningful* event for the human person.

Although these criteria are valid for the entire ministry of the word, here they are developed in relation to catechesis.

The christocentricity of the Gospel message

98. Jesus Christ not only transmits the word of God: he *is* the Word of God. Catechesis is therefore completely tied to him. Thus what must characterize the message transmitted by catechesis is, above all, its "christocentricity".[14] This may be understood in various senses.

– It means, firstly, that "at the heart of catechesis we find, in essence, a person, the Person of Jesus of Nazareth, the only Son of the Father, full of grace and truth".[15] In reality, the fundamental task of catechesis is to present Christ and everything in relation to him. This explicitly promotes the following of Jesus and communion with him; every element of the message tends to this.

– Secondly, christocentricity means that Christ is the "centre of salvation history",[16] presented by catechesis. He is indeed the final event toward which all salvation history converges. He, who came "in the fullness of time" is "the key, the centre and end of all human history".[17] The catechetical message helps the Christian to locate himself in history and to insert himself into it, by showing that Christ is the ultimate meaning of this history.

– Christocentricity, moreover, means that the Gospel message does not come from man, but is the Word of God. The Church, and in her name, every catechist can say with truth: "my teaching is not from myself: it comes from the one who sent me" (*John* 7,16). Thus all that is transmitted by catechesis is "the teaching of Jesus Christ, the truth that he communicates, or more precisely, the Truth that he is".[18] Christocentricity obliges

[14] Cf. CCC 426-429; CT 5-6; DCG (1971) 40.
[15] CT 5.
[16] DCG (1971) 41a; cf. DCG (1971) 39, 40, 44.
[17] *GS* 10.
[18] CT 6.

catechesis to transmit what Jesus teaches about God, man, happiness, the moral life, death etc. without in any way changing his thought.[19]

The Gospels, which narrate the life of Jesus, are central to the catechetical message. They are themselves endowed with a "catechetical structure".[20] They express the teaching which was proposed to the first Christian communities, and which also transmits the life of Jesus, his message and his saving actions. In catechesis, "the four Gospels occupy a central place because Christ Jesus is their centre".[21]

The trinitarian christocentricity of the Gospel message

99. The Word of God, incarnate in Jesus of Nazareth, Son of the Blessed Virgin Mary, is the Word of the Father who speaks to the world through his Spirit. Jesus constantly refers to the Father, of whom he knows he is the Only Son, and to the Holy Spirit, by whom he knows he is anointed. He is 'the Way' that leads to the innermost mystery of God.[22] The christocentricity of catechesis, in order of its internal dynamic, leads to confession of faith in God, Father, Son and Holy Spirit.

It is essentially a trinitarian christocentricity. Christians, at Baptism, are configured to Christ, "One of the Trinity",[23] and constituted "sons in the Son", in communion with the Father and the Holy Spirit. Their faith is, therefore, radically Trinitari-

---

[19] Cf. *1 Cor* 15:1-4; EN 15e, f.
[20] CT 11b.
[21] CCC 139.
[22] Cf. *Jn* 14:6.
[23] The term 'one of the Trinity' was used by the Fifth Ecumenical Council (Constantinople 533): cf. CONSTANTINOPOLITANUM II, Session VIII, can. 4, *Dz* 424. It is also used in CCC 468.

an. "The mystery of the Most Holy Trinity is the central mystery of Christian faith and life".[24]

100. The trinitarian christocentricity of the Gospel message leads catechesis to attend amongst others, to the following points.

– The internal structure of catechesis: every mode of presentation must always be christocentric-trinitarian: "Through Christ to the Father in the Holy Spirit".[25] "If catechesis lacks these three elements or neglects their close relationship, the Christian message can certainly lose its proper character".[26]

– Following the pedagogy of Jesus in revelation of the Father, of himself as the Son, and of the Holy Spirit, catechesis shows the most intimate life of God, starting with his salvific works for the good of humanity.[27] The works of God reveal who he is and the mystery of his inner Being throws light on all of his works. It is analogous with human relationships: people reveal themselves by their actions and, the more deeply we know them, the better we understand what they do.[28]

– The presentation of the innermost being of God, revealed by Jesus, the mystery of being one in essence and three in Person, has vital implications for the lives of human beings. To confess belief in one God means, that "man should not submit his personal freedom in an absolute manner to any earthly power".[29] It also implies that humanity, made in the image and likeness of God who is a "communion of persons", is called to be a fraternal society, comprised of sons and daughters of the same Father,

---

[24] CCC 234; cf. CCC 2157.
[25] DCG (1971) 41; cfr. *Eph* 2:18.
[26] Cf. DCG (1971) 41.
[27] Cf. CCC 258, 236 and 259.
[28] Cf. CCC 236.
[29] CCC 450.

and equal in personal dignity.[30] The human and social implications of the Christian concept of God are immense. The Church, in professing her faith in the Trinity and by proclaiming it to the world, understands herself as "a people gathered together in the unity of the Father, Son and Holy Spirit".[31]

A message proclaiming salvation

101. The message of Jesus about God is Good News for humanity. Jesus proclaimed the Kingdom of God;[32] a new and definitive intervention by God, with a transforming power equal and even superior to his creation of the world.[33] In this sense, "Christ proclaims salvation as the outstanding element and, as it were, the central point of his Good News. This is the great gift of God which is to be considered as comprising not merely liberation from all those things by which man is oppressed, but especially liberation from sin and from the domination of the evil one, a liberation which incorporates that gladness enjoyed by every man who knows God and is known by him, who sees God and who surrenders himself trustingly to him".[34] Catechesis transmits this message of the Kingdom, so central to the preaching of Jesus. In doing so, the message "is gradually deepened, devel-

---

[30] Cf. CCC 1878; CCC 1702. SRS uses the term model of unity when referring to this question. CCC 2845 calls the communion of the Blessed Trinity "the source and criterion of truth in every relationship".

[31] The term comes from St Cyprian "De orat. dom.", 23; PL, 4:553; LG 4b.

[32] Cf. EN 11-14; RM 12-20; cf. CCC 541-556.

[33] In the liturgy of the Church it is expressed in the Easter Vigil: "Almighty and eternal God you created all things in wonderful beauty and order. Help us now to perceive how still more wonderful is the new creation by which in the fullness of time you redeemed your people through the sacrifice of our Passover, Jesus Christ, who lives and reigns forever and ever" (Missale Romanum, Easter Vigil, prayer after the first reading).

[34] EN 9.

oped in its implicit consequences",[35] and thus manifests its great repercussions for man and the world.

102. In its drawing out the Gospel kerygma of Jesus, catechesis underlines the following basic aspects:

– Jesus, with the Kingdom, proclaims and reveals that God is not a distant inaccessible Being, "a remote power without a name" [36] but a Father, who is present among his creatures and whose power is his love. This testimony about God as Father, offered in a simple and direct manner, is fundamental to catechesis.

– Jesus shows, at the same time, that God, with the coming of his Kingdom offers the gift of integral salvation, frees from sin, brings one to communion with the Father, grants divine sonship, and in conquering death, promises eternal life.[37] This complete salvation is at once, immanent and eschatological, because "it has its beginning certainly in this life, but which achieves its consummation in eternity".[38]

– Jesus, in announcing the Kingdom, proclaims the justice of God: he proclaims God's judgement and our responsibility. The proclamation of this judgement, with its power to form consciences, is a central element in the Gospel, and Good News for the world: for those who suffer the denial of justice and for those who struggle to re-instate it; for those who have known love and existence in solidarity, because penance and forgiveness are possible, since in the Cross of Christ we all receive redemption from sin. The call to conversion and belief in the Gospel of

---

[35] CT 25.

[36] EN 26.

[37] This gift of Salvation confers on us, *"justification"* by means of the grace of faith and of the Church's Sacraments, This grace frees us from sin and introduces us to communion with God" (LC 52).

[38] EN 27.

the Kingdom—a Kingdom of justice, love and peace, and in whose light we shall be judged—is fundamental for catechesis.

– Jesus declares that the Kingdom of God is inaugurated in him, in his very person.[39] He reveals, in fact, that he himself, constituted as Lord, assumes the realization of the Kingdom until he consigns it, upon completion, to the Father when he comes again in glory.[40] "Here on earth the Kingdom is mysteriously present; when the Lord comes it will enter into its perfection".[41]

– Jesus shows, equally, that the community of his disciples, the Church, "is, on earth, the seed and the beginning of that Kingdom"[42] and, like leaven in the dough, what she desires is that the Kingdom of God grow in the world like a great tree, giving shelter to all peoples and cultures. "The Church is effectively and concretely at the service of the Kingdom".[43]

– Finally, Jesus manifests that the history of humanity is not journeying towards nothingness, but, with its aspects of both grace and sin, is in him taken up by God and transformed. In its present pilgrimage towards the Father's house, it already offers a foretaste of the world to come, where, assumed and purified, it will reach perfection. "Accordingly, evangelization will include a prophetic proclamation of another's life, that is of man's sublime and eternal vocation. This vocation is at once connected with and distinct from his present state".[44]

---

[39] Cf. LG 3 and 5.
[40] Cf. RM 16.
[41] GS 39.
[42] LG 5.
[43] RM 20.
[44] EN 28.

A message of liberation

103. The Good News of the Kingdom of God, which proclaims salvation, includes a "message of liberation".[45] In preaching this Kingdom, Jesus addressed the poor in a very special way: "Blessed are you poor, yours is the kingdom of God. Blessed are you that hunger now, for you shall be satisfied. Blessed are you that weep now, for you shall laugh" (*Lk* 6,20-21) The Beatitudes of Jesus, addressed to those who suffer, are an eschatological proclamation of the salvation which the Kingdom brings. They note that painful experience to which the Gospel is so particularly sensitive: poverty, hunger and the suffering of humanity. The community of the disciples of Jesus, the Church, shares today the same sensitivity as the Master himself showed them. With great sorrow she turns her attention to those "peoples who, as we all know, are striving with all their power and energy to overcome all those circumstances which compel them to live on the border line of existence: hunger, chronic epidemics, illiteracy, poverty, injustice between nations... economic and cultural neo-colonialism".[46] All forms of poverty, "not only economic but also cultural and religious"[47] are a source of concern for the Church.

As an important dimension of her mission, "the Church is duty bound—as her bishops have insisted—to proclaim the liberation of these hundreds of millions of people, since very many of them are her children. She has the duty of helping this liberation, of bearing witness on its behalf and of assuring its full development".[48]

---

[45] Cf. EN 30-35.
[46] EN 30.
[47] CA 57; cf. CCC 2444.
[48] EN 30.

104.   To prepare Christians for this task, catechesis is attentive, amongst other things, to the following aspects:

– it shall situate the message of liberation in the prospective of the "specifically religious objective of evangelization",[49] since it would lose its raison d'être "if it were divorced from the religious basis by which it is sustained which is the kingdom of God in its full theological sense;[50] thus, the message of liberation "cannot be confined to any restricted sphere whether it be economic, political, social or doctrinal. It must embrace the whole man in all his aspects and components, extending to his relation to the absolute, even to the Absolute which is God";[51]

– catechesis, in the ambit of moral education, shall present Christian social morality as a demand and consequence of the "radical liberation worked by Christ";[52] in effect, the Good News which Christians profess with hearts full of hope is: Christ has liberated the world and continues to liberate it; this is the source of Christian praxis, which is the fulfilment of the great commandment of love;

– at the same time, in the task of initiating mission, catechesis shall arouse in catechumens and those receiving catechesis "a preferential option for the poor",[53] which "far from being a sign of individualism or sectarianism, makes manifest the universality of the Church's nature and mission. This option is not exclu-

---

[49] EN 32; cf. SRS 41 and RM 58.
[50] EN 32.
[51] EN 33. Cf. LC. This Instruction is an obligatory point of reference for catechesis.
[52] LC 71.
[53] SRS 42; CA 57; LC 68. Cf. CCC 2443-2449.

sive" [54] but implies "a commitment to justice, according to each individual's role, vocation and circumstances". [55]

The ecclesial nature of the Gospel message

105.   The ecclesial nature of catechesis confers on the transmitted Gospel message an inherent ecclesial character. Catechesis originates in the Church's confession of faith and leads to the profession of faith of the catechumen and those to be catechized. The first official word of the Church addressed to those about to be baptized, having called them by name, is: "What do you ask of God's Church?" The candidates' reply is *"Faith"*. [56] The catechumen who has discovered the Gospel and desires to know it better, realizes that it lives in the hearts of believers. Catechesis is nothing other than the process of transmitting the Gospel, as the Christian community has received it, understands it, celebrates it, lives it and communicates it in many ways.

Hence, when catechesis transmits the mystery of Christ, the faith of the whole people of God echoes in its message throughout the course of history: the faith received by the Apostles from Christ himself and under the action of the Holy Spirit; that of the martyrs who have borne witness to it and still bear witness to it by their blood; that of the saints who have lived it and live it profoundly; that of the Fathers and doctors of the Church who have taught it brilliantly; that of the missionaries who proclaim it incessantly; that of theologians who help to understand it better; that of pastors who conserve it with zeal and love and who interpret it authentically. In truth, there is present in catech-

---

[54] LC 68.
[55] SRS 41; cf. LC 77. For its part the 1971 Synod devoted attention to a theme of fundamental importance to catechesis: Education in Justice (III, 2). Cf. Documents of the Synod of Bishops, II De Iustitia in mundo III, 835-937.
[56] RCIA 75; cf. CCC 1253.

esis the faith of all those who believe and allow themselves to be
guided by the Holy Spirit.

106.   This faith, transmitted by the ecclesial community, is one.
Although the disciples of Jesus Christ form a community dis-
persed throughout the whole world, and even though catechesis
transmits the faith in many different cultural idioms, the Gospel
which is handed on is one. The confession of faith is the same.
There is only one Baptism: "one Lord, one Faith, one Baptism
one God and Father of us all" (*Eph* 4,5). Catechesis, in the
Church, therefore, is that service which introduces catechumens
and those to be catechized to the unity of the profession of
faith.[57] By its very nature, it nourishes the bond of unity [58] and
brings about an awareness of belonging to a great community
which cannot be limited by space or time: "From Abel the just
to the last of the chosen ones to the end of the earth, to the
close of the age.[59]

The historical character of the mystery of salvation

107.   The confession of faith of the disciples of Jesus Christ
springs from a pilgrim Church which has been sent on mission.
It is not yet that of the glorious proclamation of the journey's
end; rather, it is one which corresponds to the *"times of the
Church"*.[60] The *"economy of Salvation"* has thus an historical character as it is realized in time: *"...in time past it began, made*

---

[57] Cf. CCC 172-175 where, inspired by St Irenaeus of Lyon there is an analysis of all
the riches contained in the reality of one faith.

[58] CCC 815: "...the unity of the pilgrim Church is also assured by visible bonds of
communion: profession of one faith received from the apostles; common celebration of divine worship, especially of the sacraments; apostolic succession through
the sacrament of Holy Orders, maintaining the fraternal concord of God's family".

[59] EN 61, which takes up St Gregory the Great and the Didaché.

[60] CCC 1076.

progress, and in Christ reached its highest point; in the present time it displays its force and awaits its consummation in the future.[61] For this reason, the Church, in transmitting today the Christian message, begins with the living awareness which she carries of it, has a constant "memory" of the saving events of the past and makes them known. In the light of these, she interprets the present events of human history, where the Spirit of God is continually renewing the face of the earth, and she awaits with faith for the Lord's coming. In Patristic catechesis, the narration *(narratio)* of the wonderful deeds of God and the awaiting *(expectatio)* of Christ's return always accompanied the exposition of the mysteries of faith.[62]

108.   The historical character of the Christian message requires that catechesis attend to the following points:

– presentation of salvation history by means of Biblical catechesis so as to make known the "deeds and the words" with which God has revealed himself to man: the great stages of the Old Testament by which he prepared the journey of the Gospel; [63] the life of Jesus, Son of God, born of the Virgin Mary who by his actions and teaching brought Revelation to completion; [64] the history of the Church which transmits Revelation: this history, read within the perspective of faith, is a fundamental part of the content of catechesis;

---

[61] DCG (1971) 44.

[62] The Fathers basing the content of catechesis on the narration of the events of salvation, wish to root Christianity in time by showing that it was a salvation history and not a mere religious philosophy. They also wished to emphasize that Christ was the centre of this history.

[63] CCC 54-64. At this point the catechism deals with the most important phases of revelation and in them the idea of Covenant is a key concept. These texts are a fundamental reference for biblical catechesis. Cf. CCC 1081 and 1093.

[64] Cf. DV 4.

– in explaining the Creed and the content of Christian morality by means of doctrinal catechesis, the Gospel message should illuminate the 'today' of the history of salvation; indeed, "...in this way the ministry of the Word not only recalls the revelation of God's wonders which was made in time...but at the same time, in the light of this revelation, interprets human life in our age, the signs of the times, and the things of this world, for the plan of God works in these for the salvation of men"; [65]

– it should situate the sacraments within the history of salvation by means of a mystagogy which "...re-lives the great events of salvation history in the 'today' of her liturgy"; [66] reference to the historico-salvific 'today' is essential to such catechesis, and thus helps catechumens and those to be catechized "to open themselves to this 'spiritual' understanding of the economy of Salvation..."; [67]

– the *"deeds and words"* of Revelation point to the *"mystery contained in them"*; [68] catechesis helps to make the passage from sign to mystery; it leads to the discovery of the mystery of the Son of God behind his humanity; behind the history of the Church, it uncovers the mystery of her being the "sacrament of salvation;" behind the "signs of the times", it encounters the traces of God's presence and plan: catechesis, thus, shall exhibit that knowledge which is typical of faith, which "is knowledge through signs".[69]

---

[65] DCG (1971) 11.

[66] CCC 1095. Cf. CCC 1075; CCC 1116; cf. CCC 129-130 and 1093-1094.

[67] CCC 1095. CCC 1075 indicates the inductive nature of this "mystagogical catechesis" since it proceeds "from the visible to the invisible, from the sign to the thing signified, from the 'sacraments' to the 'mysteries'".

[68] DV 2.

[69] DCG (1971) 72; cf. CCC 39-43.

Inculturation of the Gospel message [70]

109. The Word of God became man, a concrete man, in space and time and rooted in a specific culture: "Christ by his incarnation committed himself to the particular social and cultural circumstances of the men among whom he lived".[71] This is the original "inculturation" of the word of God and is the model of all evangelization by the Church, "called to bring the power of the Gospel into the very heart of culture and cultures".[72]

'Inculturation' [73] of the faith, whereby in a wonderful exchange are comprised, "all the riches of the nations which have been given to Christ as an inheritance",[74] it is a profound and global process and a slow journey.[75] It is not simply an external adaptation designed to make the Christian message more attractive or superficially decorative. On the contrary, it means the penetration of the deepest strata of persons and peoples by the Gospel which touches them deeply, "going to the very centre and roots" [76] of their cultures.

In this work of inculturation, however, the Christian community must discern, on the one hand, which riches to "take" [77] up as compatible with the faith; on the other, it must seek to "puri-

---

[70] Cf. Part IV, chp 5.
[71] AG 10; cf. AG 22a.
[72] CT 53; cf. EN 20.
[73] The term "inculturation" is taken from diverse documents of the Magisterium. See CT 53; RM 52-54. The concept of culture, either in a general or an ethnological or sociological sense is clarified in GS 53. Cf. also ChL 44a.
[74] AG 22a; cf. LG 13 and 17; GS 53-62; DCG (1971) 37.
[75] Cf. RM 52b which speaks of the "long time" required for inculturation.
[76] EN 20; cf. EN 63; RM 52.
[77] LG 13 uses the expression *"to foster and to take (fovet et assumit)"*.

fy" [78] and "transform" [79] those criteria, modes of thought and life-
styles which are contrary to the Kingdom of God. Such discernment is governed by two basic principles: "compatibility with the
Gospel and communion with the universal Church".[80] All of the
people of God must be involved in this process which "...needs
to take place gradually, in such a way that it really is an expression of the community's Christian experience".[81]

110.   In this inculturation of the faith, there are different concrete tasks for catechesis. Amongst these mention must be made of:

– looking to the ecclesial community as the principal factor
of inculturation: an expression and efficient instrument of this
task is represented by the catechist who, with a profound religious sense, also possesses a living social conscience and is well
rooted in his cultural environment; [82]

– drawing up local catechisms which respond to the demands
of different cultures [83] and which present the Gospel in relation
to the hopes, questions and problems which these cultures present;

– making the Catechumenate and catechetical institutes into
"centres of inculturation", incorporating, with discernment, the
language, symbols, and values of the cultures in which the catechumens and those to be catechized live;

– presenting the Christian message in such a way as to prepare those who are to proclaim the Gospel to be capable "of
giving reasons for their hope" (*1 Pt* 3,15) in cultures often pagan

---

[78] LG 13 expresses it in this way: *"she purifies, strengthens and elevates them (sanare, elevare et consummare)"*.
[79] EN 19 affirms: *"to acquire and almost to overturn"*.
[80] RM 54a.
[81] RM 54b.
[82] Cf. *Guide for catechists*, 12.
[83] Cf. CCC 24.

or post-Christian: effective apologetics to assist the faith-culture dialogue is indispensable today.

The integrity of the Gospel message

111.   In its task of inculturating the faith, catechesis must transmit the Gospel message in its integrity and purity. Jesus proclaimed the Gospel integrally: " ..because I have made known to you all that I have heard from my Father" (*Jn* 15,15) This same integrity is demanded by Christ of his disciples in his sending them on mission to preach the Gospel: "...and teaching them to observe all that I have commanded you" (*Mt* 28,19). A fundamental principle of catechesis, therefore, is that of safeguarding the integrity of the message and avoiding any partial or distorted presentation: "In order that the sacrificial offering of his or her faith should be perfect, the person who becomes a disciple of Christ has the right to receive 'the words of faith,' not in mutilated, falsified or diminished form but whole and entire, in all its rigour and vigour".[84]

112.   Two closely connected dimensions underlie this criterion.

– The *integral* presentation of the Gospel message, without ignoring certain fundamental elements, or without operating a selectivity with regard to the deposit of faith.[85] Catechesis, on the contrary, "must take diligent care faithfully to present the entire treasure of the Christian message".[86] This is accomplished, gradually, by following the example of the divine pedagogy with which God revealed himself progressively and gradually. Integrity must also be accompanied by adaptation. Consequently catechesis starts out with a simple proposition of the integral structure of

---

[84] CT 30.
[85] *Ibid.*
[86] DCG (1971) 38a.

the Christian message, and proceeds to explain it in a manner adapted to the capacity of those being catechized. Without restricting itself to this initial exposition, it gradually and increasingly proposes the Christian message more amply and with greater explicitness, in accordance with the capacity of those being catechized and with the proper character of catechesis.[87] These two levels of the integral exposition of the Gospel message are called: *intensive integrity* and *"extensive integrity"*.

 – The presentation of the authentic Gospel message, in all of its purity, without reducing idemands for fear of rejection and without imposing heavy burdens which it does not impose, since the yoke of Jesus is light.[88] The criterion of authenticity is closely connected with that of inculturation since the latter is concerned to "translate" [89] the essentials of the Gospel message into a definite cultural language. There is always tension in this necessary task: "Evangelization will lose much of its power and efficacy if it does not take into consideration the people to whom it is addressed.". however "it may lose its very nature and savour if on the pretext of transposing its content into another language that content is rendered meaningless or is corrupted...[90]

113.   In the complex relationship between inculturation and the integrity of the Christian message, the criterion to be applied is a Gospel attitude of "a missionary openness to the integral salvation of the world".[91] This must always unite acceptance of truly human and religious values with the missionary task of proclaiming the whole truth of the Gospel, without falling either into closed inflexibility or into facile accommodations which enfeeble

[87] DCG (1971) 38b.
[88] Cf. *Mt* 11:30.
[89] EN 63 uses the expressions *"transferre"* and *"traslatio"*; cf. RM 53b.
[90] EN 63c; cf. CT 53c and CT 31.
[91] Synod 1985, II, D, 3; cf. EN 65.

the Gospel and secularize the Church. Gospel authenticity excludes both of these attitudes which are contrary to the true meaning of mission.

A comprehensive and hierarchical message

114.　This message transmitted by catechetics has a "comprehensive hierarchical character",[92] which constitutes a coherent and vital synthesis of the faith. This is organized around the mystery of the Most Holy Trinity, in a christocentric perspective, because this is "the source of all the other mysteries of faith, the light that enlightens them".[93] Starting with this point, the harmony of the overall message requires a "hierarchy of truths",[94] in so far as the connection between each one of these and the foundation of the faith differs. Nevertheless, this hierarchy "does not mean that some truths pertain to Faith itself less than others, but rather that some truths are based on others as of a higher priority and are illumined by them".[95]

115.　All aspects and dimensions of the Christian message participate in this hierarchical system.

– The history of salvation, recounting the "marvels of God" (mirabilia Dei), what He has done, continues to do and will do in the future for us, is organized in reference to Jesus Christ, the "centre of salvation history".[96] The preparation for the Gospel in the Old Testament, the fullness of Revelation in Jesus Christ, and the time of the Church, provide the structure of all salvation his-

---

[92] CT 31 which expounds the integrity and organization of the message; cf. DCG (1971) 39 and 43.
[93] CCC 234.
[94] UR 11.
[95] DCG (1971) 43.
[96] DCG (1971) 41.

tory of which creation and eschatology are its beginning and its end.

– The Apostles' Creed demonstrates how the Church has always desired to present the Christian mystery in a vital synthesis. This Creed is a synthesis of and a key to reading all of the Church's doctrine, which is hierarchically ordered around it. [97]

– The sacraments, which, like regenerating forces, spring from the paschal mystery of Jesus Christ, are also a whole. They form "an organic whole in which each particular sacrament has its own vital place". [98] In this whole, the Holy Eucharist occupies a unique place to which all of the other sacraments are ordained. The Eucharist is to be presented as the "sacrament of sacraments". [99]

– The double commandment of love of God and neighbour is—in the moral message—a hierarchy of values which Jesus himself established: "On these two commandments depend all the Law and the Prophets" (*Mt* 22,40). The love of God and neighbour, which sum up the Decalogue, are lived in the spirit of the Beatitudes and constitute the magna carta of the Christian life proclaimed by Jesus in the Sermon on the Mount. [100]

– The Our Father gathers up the essence of the Gospel. It synthesizes and hierarchically structures the immense riches of

[97] St Cyril of Jerusalem affirms with regard to the Creed: "This synthesis of faith was not made to accord with human opinions but rather what was of the greatest importance was gathered from all the Scriptures, to present the one teaching of the faith in its entirety. And just as a mustard seed contains a great number of branches in a tiny grain, so too the summary of faith encompassed in a few words the whole knowledge of the true religion contained in the Old and New Testaments".

[98] CCC 1211.

[99] *Ibid.*

[100] St Augustine presents the Sermon on the Mount as "the perfect charter of the Christian life and contains all the appropriate precepts necessary to guide it" (*De Sermone Domini in Monte* I, 1; PL 34, 1229-1231); cf. EN 8.

prayer contained in Sacred Scripture and in all of the Church's life. This prayer, given by Jesus to his disciples, makes clear the childlike trust and the deepest desires with which one can turn to God.[101]

A meaningful message for the human person

116. The Word of God, in becoming man, assumed human nature in everything, except sin. In this way Jesus Christ, who is "the image of the invisible God", (*Col* 1,15) is also the perfect man. From this it follows that "in reality it is only in the mystery of the Word made flesh that the mystery of man truly becomes clear".[102]

Catechesis, in presenting the Christian message, not only shows who God is and what his saving plan is, but, as Jesus himself did, it reveals man to man and makes him more aware of his sublime vocation.[103] Revelation, in fact, "... is not... isolated from life or artificially juxtaposed to it. It is concerned with the ultimate meaning of life and it illumines the whole of life with the light of the Gospel, to inspire it or to question it".[104]

The relationship between the Christian message and human experience is not a simple methodological question. It springs from the very end of catechesis, which seeks to put the human person in communion with Jesus Christ. In his earthly life he lived his humanity fully: "He worked with human hands, he thought with a human mind, he acted with a human will, and

---

[101] The Our Father is, in truth, the summing up of the entire Gospel (TERTULLIAN, *De oratione*, 1, 6). "*Go through all the prayers in the Scriptures and I do not believe that it is possible to find anyone, anywhere, that is not included in the Lord's Prayer.* (ST AUGUSTINE, *Epistolas*, 130, 12; PL, 33, 502); cf. CCC 2761.

[102] GS 22a.

[103] Cf. *Ibid.*

[104] CT 22c; cf. EN 29.

with a human heart he loved".[105] Therefore, "Christ enables us to live in him all that he himself lived, and he lives it in us".[106] Catechesis operates through this identity of human experience between Jesus the Master and his disciple and teaches to think like him, to act like him, to love like him.[107] To live communion with Christ is to experience the new life of grace.[108]

117. For this reason, catechesis is eminently christological in presenting the Christian message and should therefore "be concerned with making men attentive to their more significant experiences, both personal and social; it also has the duty of placing under the light of the Gospel, the questions which arise from those experiences so that there may be stimulated within men a right desire to transform their ways of life".[109] In this sense:

– in first evangelization, proper to the pre-catechumenate or to pre-catechesis, the proclamation of the Gospel shall always be done in close connection with human nature and its aspirations, and will show how the Gospel fully satisfies the human heart; [110]

– in biblical catechesis, it shall help to interpret present-day human life in the light of the experiences of the people of Israel, of Jesus Christ and the ecclesial community, in which the Spirit of the Risen Jesus continually lives and works;

– in explaining the Creed, catechesis shall show how the great themes of the faith (creation, original sin, Incarnation, Easter, Pentecost, eschatology) are always sources of life and light for the human being;

---

[105] GS 22b.
[106] CCC 521; cf. CCC 519-521.
[107] Cf. CT 20b.
[108] Cf. *Rm* 6:4.
[109] DCG (1971) 74; cf. CT 29.
[110] Cf. AG 8a.

– moral catechesis, in presenting what makes life worthy of the Gospel [111] and in promoting the Beatitudes as the spirit that must permeate the Decalogue, shall root them in the human virtues present in the heart of man; [112]

– liturgical catechesis shall make constant reference to the great human experiences represented by the signs and symbols of liturgical actions originating in Jewish and Christian culture. [113]

Methodological principle for the presentation of the message [114]

118.   The norms and criteria indicated in this chapter and those concerning the "exposition of the content of catechesis, must be applied in the various forms of catechesis, that is to say, in biblical and liturgical catechesis, in doctrinal summaries, in the interpretation of the conditions of human existence and so on. [115]

From these, however, it is not possible to deduce the order that should be observed in the exposition of catechetical content. Indeed, "it can happen that in the present situation of catechesis reasons of method or pedagogy may suggest that the communication of the riches of the content of catechesis should be organized in one way rather than another". [116] It is possible to begin with God so as to arrive at Christ, and vice versa. Equally, it is possible to start with man and come to God, and conversely. The selection of a particular order for presenting the message is conditioned by circumstances, and by the faith level of those to be catechized. It will always be necessary to elaborate with care that pedagogical method which is most appropriate to the cir-

---

[111] Cf. *Phil* 1:27.
[112] Cf. CCC 1697.
[113] Cf. CCC 1145-1152 concerning the importance of signs and symbols in liturgical action.
[114] Cf. part III, chapter 2.
[115] DCG (1971) 46.
[116] CT 31.

cumstances of an ecclesial community or of those to whom catechesis is specifically addressed. Hence derives the need to inves-
tigate correctly in order to find those means which best respond
to different situations.

It is a matter for Bishops to draw up more particular norms
for this and to apply them by means of Catechetical Directories
and catechisms which cater for different ages and cultural conditions, as well as in other ways deemed more appropriate.[117]

---

[117] Cf. CIC 775, §§ 1-3.

CHAPTER II

"This is our faith
this is the faith of the Church"

"All Scripture is inspired by God and profitable for teaching, for reproof, for correction, and for training in righteousness" (2 Thess 2:15).

"So then, brethren, stand firm and hold to the tradition which you were taught by us, either by word of mouth or by letter" (2 Thess 2:15).

---

119.   This chapter reflects on the content of catechesis as presented by the Church in the syntheses of faith which are officially drawn up and presented in her catechisms. The Church has always used formulations of faith which, in short forms, contain the essentials of what she believes and lives: New Testament texts, creeds or professions of faith, liturgical formulas, Eucharistic prayers. At a later period, it was considered useful to provide more ample explicitations of the faith in organic synthesis, through the catechisms compiled in numerous local Churches in recent centuries. In two historical moments, at the Council of Trent and in our own times, it was considered opportune to furnish a comprehensive presentation of the faith in a catechism of a universal nature, which would serve as a reference point for catechesis throughout the Church. It was with this intention that Pope John Paul II promulgated the *Catechism of the Catholic Church* on 11 October 1992.

The present chapter seeks to situate these official instruments of the Church, which is what catechisms are, in relation with catechetical activity and praxis.

In the first place, it will reflect on the *Catechism of the Catholic Church* and seek to clarify its role in the overall catechesis of the Church. It will, then, analyse the need for local catechisms to adapt the content of the faith to different circumstances and cultures. Some directions will be given to assist the preparation of such catechisms. The Church, contemplating the richness of the content of faith, which the Bishops propose to the people of God and which they express like a "symphony" [1] celebrates, lives and proclaims what she believes: "This is our faith, this is the faith of the Church".

The Catechism of the Catholic Church and the General Directory for Catechesis

120. The *Catechism of the Catholic Church* and the *General Catechetical Directory* are two distinct but complementary instruments at the service of the Church's catechetical activity.

– The *Catechism of the Catholic Church* is "a statement of the Church's faith and of Catholic doctrine, attested to or illuminated by Sacred Scripture, the Apostolic Tradition and the Church's Magisterium.[2]

– The *General Directory for Catechesis* provides "the basic principles of pastoral theology taken from the Magisterium of the Church, and in a special way from the Second Vatican Council by which pastoral action in the ministry of the word can be more fittingly directed and governed".[3]

[1] Cf. FD 2d.
[2] FD 4a.
[3] DCG (1971) *Introduction*.

Both instruments, each taken in accordance with its specific nature and authority, are mutually complementary. The *Catechism of the Catholic Church* is an act of the Magisterium of the Pope, by which, in our times, in virtue of Apostolic Authority, he synthesizes normatively the totality of the Catholic faith. He offers the *Catechism of the Catholic Church*, in the first place, to the Churches as a point of reference for the authentic presentation of the content of the faith. The *Catechetical Directory,* for its part, carries that authority normally vested by the Holy See in instruments of orientation by approving them and confirming them. It is an official aid for the transmission of the Gospel message and for the whole of catechetical activity. The complementary nature of both of these instruments justifies the fact, as already mentioned in the *Preface,* that this *General Catechetical Directory* does not devote a chapter to the presentation of the contents of the faith, as was the case in the 1971 *General Catechetical Directory for Catechesis* under the title: *"The more outstanding elements of the Christian message".*[4] *Such is explained by the fact that this Directory, as far as the content of the Christian message is concerned, simply refers to the Catechism of the Catholic Church",* which is intended as a methodological norm for its concrete application. The following exposition of the *Catechism of the Catholic Church* seeks neither to summarize its contents nor to explain this instrument of the Magisterium. It simply seeks to facilitate a better understanding and use of the *Catechism of the Catholic Church* in catechetical practice.

[4] DCG (1971) Part III, chap. 2.

THE CATECHISM OF THE CATHOLIC CHURCH

Nature and purpose of the Catechism of the Catholic Church

121. The *Prologue* to the *Catechism of the Catholic Church* states its purpose: "This catechism aims at presenting an organic synthesis of the essential and fundamental contents of Catholic doctrine, as regards both faith and morals, in the light of the Second Vatican Council and the whole of the Church's Tradition".[5] The Magisterium of the Church intends to render an ecclesial service for our times with the *Catechism of the Catholic Church*, recognizing that it is:

– "a valid and legitimate instrument for *ecclesial communion*":[6] it desires to promote the bond of unity in the faith by helping the disciples of Jesus Christ to make "the profession of one faith received from the Apostles";[7]

– "a sure norm for *teaching the faith*":[8] the *Catechism of the Catholic Church* offers a clear response to the legitimate right of all the baptized to know from the Church what she has received and what she believes; it is thus an obligatory point of reference for catechesis and for the other forms of the ministry of the word.

– "a sure and authentic reference text for teaching Catholic doctrine and particularly for preparing local catechisms":[9] the *Catechism of the Catholic Church*, in fact, "is not intended to replace the local catechism (duly approved)"[10] but "to encourage and assist in the writing of new local catechisms which take into

---

[5] CCC 11.
[6] FD 4a; cf. FD 4b.
[7] CCC 815.
[8] FD 4a; cf. FD 4c.
[9] FD 1f; cf. FD 4c.
[10] FD 4d.

account various situations and cultures, while carefully preserving the unity of faith and fidelity to Catholic doctrine".[11]

The nature or character proper to this document of the Magisterium consists in the fact that it is a comprehensive synthesis of the faith and thus it is of universal value. In this, it differs from other documents of the Magisterium, which do not set out to present such a synthesis. It differs also from local Catechisms, which, within the context of ecclesial communion, are destined for the service of a particular portion of the people of God.

Structure of the Catechism of the Catholic Church

122.   The *Catechism of the Catholic Church* is structured around four fundamental dimensions of the Christian life: the profession of faith; the celebration of the liturgy; the morality of the Gospel; and prayer. These four dimensions spring from a single source, the *Christian mystery*. This is:

– the object of the faith *(Part One);*

– celebrated and communicated in liturgical actions *(Part Two);*

– present to enlighten and sustain the children of God in their actions *(Part Three);*

– the basis of our prayer, whose supreme expression is the *Our Father*, and the object of our supplication, praise and intercession *(Part Four)*;[12]

This four part structure develops the essential aspects of the faith:

– belief in the Triune God and in his saving plan;

– sanctification by him in the sacramental life;

– loving him with all one's heart and one's neighbour as oneself;

[11] *Ibid.*
[12] FD 3d.

– prayer while waiting for the coming of his Kingdom and our meeting with him face to face.

The *Catechism of the Catholic Church* thus refers to the faith as believed, celebrated, lived and prayed. It is a call to integral Christian education. The structure of the *Catechism of the Catholic Church* derives from the profound unity of the Christian life. It maintains an explicit interrelation between *"lex orandi"*, *"lex credendi"* and *"lex vivendi"*. "The Liturgy itself is prayer; the confession of faith finds its proper place in the celebration of worship. Grace, the fruit of the sacraments, is the irreplaceable condition for Christian living, just as participation in the Church's Liturgy requires faith. If faith is not expressed in works it is dead and cannot bear fruit into eternal life".[13]

Structured around the four pillars [14] which sustain the transmission of the faith (*the Creed, the Sacraments, the Decalogue, the Our Father*), the *Catechism of the Catholic Church* is presented as a doctrinal point of reference for education in the four basic tasks of catechesis,[15] and for the drawing up of local catechisms. It does not, however, impose a predetermined configuration on the one or on the other. "The best structure for catechesis must be one which is suitable to particular concrete circumstances and cannot be established for the entire Church by a common catechism".[16] Perfect fidelity to Catholic doctrine is compatible with a rich diversity of presentation.

---

[13] FD 2e.
[14] Cf.CCC 13.
[15] Cf. Part One, chap. 3.
[16] H.E. JOSEPH Cardinal RATZINGER, *Il Catechismo della Chiesa Cattolica e l'otttsimo dei redenti in* J. RATZINGER-C. SCHÖNBORN, *Brief introduction to the Catechism of the Catholic Church* (original title *Kleine Hinfürung zum Catechismus der Katolischen Kirche,* München 1993) Roma 1994, pp. 26-27.

The inspiration of the Catechism of the Catholic Church: trinitarian christocentricity and the nobility of the vocation of the human person

123. The axis of the *Catechism of the Catholic Church* is Jesus Christ, "the Way, the Truth and the Life" (*Jn* 14,6). Centred on him, it is orientated in two directions: toward God and toward the human person.

– The mystery of the Triune God and of his economy of salvation inspires and organizes the internal structure of the *Catechism of the Catholic Church* in general and in particular. The profession of faith, the liturgy, the morality of the Gospel and prayer in the *Catechism of the Catholic Church* all have a trinitarian inspiration, which runs through the entire work.[17]

– The mystery of the human person is presented throughout the *Catechism of the Catholic Church* and specifically in some particularly significant chapters: "Man is capable of God", "The creation of Man", "The Son of God became Man", "The vocation of Man and life in the Spirit"... and others.[18] This doctrine, contemplated in the light of the humanity of Jesus, the perfect man, demonstrates the highest vocation and the ideal of perfection to which every human person is called.

Indeed, the doctrine of the *Catechism of the Catholic Church* can be distilled into the following remark of the Council: "Jesus Christ, by revealing the mystery of the Father and of his love, fully reveals man to himself and brings to light his most high calling".[19]

---

[17] Cf. CCC 189-190; 1077-1109; 1693-1695; 2564; etc.
[18] Cf. CCC 27-49; 355-379; 456-478; 1699-1756; etc.
[19] GS 22a.

The literary genre of The Catechism of the Catholic Church

124.   It is important to understand the literary genre of the *Catechism of the Catholic Church* in order to foster the role which the Church's authority gives to it in the exercise and renewal of catechetical activity in our time. The principal characteristics of this follow:

– The *Catechism of the Catholic Church* is above all a catechism; that is to say, an official text of the Church's Magisterium, which authoritatively gathers in a precise form, and in an organic synthesis the events and fundamental salvific truths which express the faith common to the People of God and which constitute the indispensable basic reference for catechesis.

– In virtue of being a catechism, the *Catechism of the Catholic Church* collects all that is fundamental and common to the Christian life without "presenting as doctrines of the faith special interpretations which are only private opinions or the views of some theological school".[20]

– The *Catechism of the Catholic Church* is, moreover, a catechism of a universal nature and is offered to the entire Church. It presents an updated synthesis of the faith which incorporates the doctrine of the Second Vatican Council as well as the religious and moral concerns of our times. However, "by design this Catechism does not set out to provide the adaptation of doctrinal presentations and the catechetical methods required by the differences of culture, age, spiritual maturity and social and ecclesial condition amongst all those to whom it is addressed. Such indispensable adaptations are the responsibility of particular catechisms and, even more, of those who instruct the faithful".[21]

[20] Cf. DCG (1971) 119.
[21] CCC 24.

The Deposit of Faith and the Catechism of the Catholic Church

125. The Second Vatican Council set as one of its principal tasks the "better conservation and presentation of the precious deposit of Christian doctrine so as to render it more accessible to Christ's faithful and to all men of good will". The content of that deposit is the word of God which is safeguarded in the Church. The Magisterium of the Church, having decided to draw up "a reference text" for the teaching of the faith, has chosen from this precious treasure "things new and old" which it considers suitable for accomplishing this task. The *Catechism of the Catholic Church* thus constitutes a fundamental service by encouraging the proclamation of the Gospel and the teaching of the faith, which both draw their message from Tradition and Sacred Scripture entrusted to the Church, so as to achieve this function with complete authenticity. The *Catechism of the Catholic Church* is not the only source of catechesis, since as an act of the Magisterium, "it is not superior to the word of God but at its service". However it is a particularly authentic act of interpretation of that word, such that the Gospel may be proclaimed and transmitted in all its truth and purity.

126. In the light of this relationship between the *Catechism of the Catholic Church* and the *"deposit of faith"*, it may be useful to clarify two questions of vital importance for catechesis:

— the relationship between Sacred Scripture and the *Catechism of the Catholic Church* as points of reference for the content of catechesis;

— the relationship between the catechetical tradition of the Fathers of the Church, with its rich content and its profound understanding of the catechetical process, and the *Catechism of the Catholic Church*.

Sacred Scripture, the Catechism of the Catholic Church, and Catechesis

127. The Constitution *Dei Verbum* of the Second Vatican Council emphasizes the fundamental importance of Sacred Scripture in the Church's life. Together with tradition, it is the "supreme rule of faith", since it transmits "the very word of God" and makes "to resound... the voice of the Holy Spirit".[22] For this reason the Church desires that in the ministry of the word, Sacred Scripture should have a pre-eminent position. In concrete terms, catechesis should be "an authentic introduction to *lectio divina,* that is, to a reading of the Sacred Scriptures done in accordance to the Spirit who dwells in the Church".[23] "In this sense, to describe Tradition and Scripture as sources for catechesis means that catechesis must imbibe and permeate itself with biblical and evangelical thought, spirit and attitudes by constant contact with them. It also means that catechesis will be as rich and as effective only to the extent that these texts are read with the mind and heart of the Church".[24] In this ecclesial reading of the Scriptures, done in the light of Tradition, the *Catechism of the Catholic Church* plays a most important role.

128. Sacred Scripture and the *Catechism of the Catholic Church* are presented as two basic sources of inspiration for all catechetical activity in our time.

– Sacred Scripture as, "the word of God written under the inspiration of the Holy Spirit",[25] and the *Catechism of the Catholic Church,* as a significant contemporary expression of the living

---

[22] DV 21.
[23] MPD 9c. Cf. PONTIFICAL BIBLICAL COMMISSION, *The interpretation of the Bible in the Church,* IV, c, 3 l.c.
[24] CT 27; cf. Synod 1985, II B, a, 1.
[25] DV 9.

Tradition of the Church and a sure orm for teaching the faith, are called, each in its own way and according to its specific authority, to nourish catechesis in the Church of today.

– Catechesis transmits the content of the word of God according to the two modalities whereby the Church possesses it, interiorizes it and lives it: as a narration of the history of salvation and as an explicitation of the Creed. Both Sacred Scripture and the *Catechism of the Catholic Church* must inform biblical as well as doctrinal catechesis so that they become true vehicles of the content of God's word.

– In the ordinary development of catechesis it is important that catechumens and those to be catechized can have trust in both Sacred Scripture and the local catechism. Catechesis, by definition, is nothing other than the living and meaningful transmission of these "documents of faith".[26]

The catechetical tradition of the Fathers and the Catechism of the Catholic Church

129. The whole Tradition of the Church together with Scripture is contained in the *"deposit of faith"*. "The sayings of the holy Fathers are a witness to the life-giving presence of this Tradition, showing how its riches are poured out in the practice and life of the Church, in her belief and in her prayer".[27] With regard to this doctrinal and pastoral richness, some aspects merit special attention:

– the decisive importance which the fathers attribute to the baptismal catechumenate in the structure of the particular churches;

---

[26] Cf. MPD 9.
[27] DV 8c.

– the gradual and progressive conception of Christian formation, arranged in stages: [28] The fathers model the catechumenate on the divine pedagogy; in the catechumenal process the catechumen, like the people of Israel, goes through a journey to arrive at the promised land: Baptismal identification with Christ.[29]

– The organization of the content of catechesis in accordance with the stages of that process; in patristic catechesis a primary role is devoted to the *narration* of the history of salvation; as Lent advanced, the *Creed* and the *Our Father* were handed on to the catechumens together with their meaning and moral implications; after the celebration of the sacraments of initiation, mystagogical catechesis helped interiorize them and to savour the experience of configuration to Christ and of communion with him.

130.   The *Catechism of the Catholic Church,* for its part, brings to catechesis "the great tradition of catechisms".[30] In the richness of this tradition the following aspects deserve attention:

– The cognitive or truth dimension of the faith: this is not only living attachment to God but also assent of intellect and will; the catechisms constantly remind the Church of the need

[28] When the Second Vatican Council called for the restoration of the adult catechumenate it underlined its necessary gradual nature: "The Adult Catechumenate arranged in various stages will be re-established" (SC 64).

[29] The witness of Origen is significant: "When you abandon the darkness of idolatry and when you wish to arrive at a knowledge of the Divine Law then you begin your exodus from Egypt. When you are counted among the multitude of the catechumens, when you have started to obey the commandments of the Church, then you have crossed the Red Sea. During the sojourn in the desert, everyday, when you apply yourself to listen to the Law of God and to contemplate the face of Moses who uncovers for you the glory of the Lord. But when you arrive at the baptismal font, having crossed the Jordan, then you will enter into the Promised Land" (*Homiliae in Iesu Nave,* IV, 1: SCh 71, 149).

[30] CCC 13.

for the faithful to have an organic knowledge of the faith, however simple in form;

– An education in the faith, which is well rooted in all its sources, embraces all the different dimensions of faith profession, celebration, life and prayer.

The wealth of the patristic tradition and the tradition of catechisms comes together in the actual catechesis of the Church, enriching her in her own concept of catechesis and of its contents. These traditions bring to catechesis the seven basic elements which characterize it: the three phases in the narration of the history of salvation (the Old Testament, the life of Jesus Christ and the history of the Church) and the four pillars of its exposition (the Creed, the Sacraments, the *Decalogue* and the *Our Father*). With these seven foundation stones, both of initiatory catechesis and of continuing Christian development, various schemes and styles may be devised, in accordance with the different cultural situations of those to whom catechesis is addressed.

CATECHISMS IN THE LOCAL CHURCHES

Local Catechisms: their necessity [31]

131. The *Catechism of the Catholic Church* is given to all the faithful and to those who wish to know what the Catholic Church believes.[32] It is "meant to encourage and assist in the writing of new local catechisms, which take into account various

---

[31] This section refers exclusively to official catechisms, that is those catechisms which are proper to the diocesan bishop or Episcopal Conference (CIC 775). Non official catechisms (CIC 827) and other catechetical aids (DCG (1971) 116) will be considered in Part V, chap. 4.

[32] FD 4c.

situations and cultures, while carefully preserving the unity of faith and Catholic doctrine".[33]

Local catechisms, prepared or approved by diocesan Bishops or by Episcopal Conferences,[34] are invaluable instruments for catechesis which are "called to bring the power of the Gospel into the very heart of culture and cultures".[35] For this reason Pope John Paul II has offered a warm encouragement "to the Episcopal Conferences of the whole world to undertake, patiently but resolutely, the considerable work to be accomplished, in agreement with the Apostolic See, in order to prepare genuine catechisms which will be faithful to the essential content of Revelation and up to date in method, and which will be capable of educating the Christian generations of the future to a sturdy faith".[36]

By means of local catechisms, the Church actualizes the "divine pedagogy"[37] used by God himself in Revelation, adapting his language to our nature with thoughtful concern.[38] In local catechisms, the Church communicates the Gospel in a manner accessible to the human person so that it may be really perceived as the "Good News" of salvation. Local catechisms are palpable expressions of the wonderful "condescension"[39] of God and of his "ineffable"[40] love for the world.

---

[33] FD 4d.
[34] Cf. CIC 775.
[35] CT 53a; cf. CCC 24.
[36] CT 50.
[37] DV 15.
[38] Cf. DV 13.
[39] DV 13.
[40] DV 13. *"Ineffable kindness"*, *"providence and care"*, *"condescension"* are terms which define the divine pedagogy in Revelation. They show God's desire *to " adapt Himself"* (synkatabasis) to human beings. This same spirit should guide the redaction of local catechisms.

The literary genre of the local catechism

132. Three principal traits characterize every catechism adopted by a local Church: its official character, its organic and fundamental synthesis of the faith, and the fact that, along with Sacred Scripture, it is offered as a reference point for catechesis.

– The local catechism is an official text of the Church. In a certain sense, it makes visible the "handing on of the Creed" and the "handing on of the Our Father" to catechumens and those to be baptized. For this reason, it is an act of *tradition.* The official character of local catechisms establishes a qualitative difference from other instruments which may be useful for catechetical pedagogy *(didactic texts, non-official catechisms, catechetical guides etc.)*

– Moreover, every catechism is a synthetic and basic text, in which the events and fundamental truths of the Christian mystery are presented in an organic way and with regard to the "hierarchy of truths". The local catechism presents, in its organic structure, "an ensemble of the documents of Revelation and Christian Tradition",[41] made available in the rich diversity of "languages" in which the word of God is expressed.

– The local catechism, finally, is given as a reference point to inform catechesis. The Sacred Scriptures and the catechism are the two basic doctrinal texts for the process of catechesis and must always be to hand. While both of these texts are of the greatest importance, they are not the only texts available. Indeed, other more immediate aids are necessary.[42] It is, therefore, a valid question to ask if an official catechism should contain peda-

---

[41] DCG (1971) 119.

[42] In catechesis apart from catechetical aids there are other decisive factors: the person of the catechist, his method of transmission, the rapport between catechist and those being catechized, respect for the receptive capacity of those being catechized,

gogical elements or, on the contrary, should be limited to giving a doctrinal synthesis and a presentation of sources.

In any case, the catechism, being an instrument of catechetical activity, which is an act of communication, always reflects a certain pedagogical inspiration and must always make apparent, in its own way, the divine pedagogy.

More purely methodological questions are obviously more appropriate to other instruments.

Aspects of adaptation in a local catechism [43]

133. The *Catechism of the Catholic Church* indicates those aspects which must be taken into account when adapting or contextualizing the organic synthesis of the faith which every local catechism must offer. This synthesis of the faith must exhibit the adaptations which are required by "the differences of culture, age, spiritual maturity, and social and ecclesial conditions among all those to whom it is addressed".[44] The Second Vatican Council also emphatically affirms the need for adapting the Gospel Message: "Indeed, this kind of adaptation and preaching of the revealed word must ever be the law of all evangelization".[45] Hence:

– The local catechism must present the synthesis of the faith with reference to the particular culture in which catechumens and those to be catechized are immersed. It will, however, incorporate all those "original expressions of life, of celebrations and of thought which are Christian",[46] proper to a particular cultural

---

an atmosphere of love and faith in communication, active involvement of the Christian community, etc.
[43] Cf. part IV, chapter 1.
[44] CCC 24.
[45] GS 44.
[46] CT 53a.

tradition and are the fruits of the work and inculturation of the local Church.

– The local catechism, "faithful to the message and to the human person",[47] presents the Christian message in a meaningful way and is close to the psychology and mentality of those for whom it is intended. Consequently, it will refer clearly to the fundamental experiences of their lives.[48]

– It shall pay attention in a special way to the concrete manner in which religion is lived in a given society. It is not, for example, the same thing to prepare a catechism for a society permeated by religious indifference as it is for a profoundly religious context.[49] The relationship between belief and science must be treated with great care in every catechism.

– Problems arising from social conditions, especially those arising from its more profound structural elements (economics, politics, family) are a factor in the contextualization of a catechism. Drawing inspiration from the social teaching of the Church, the Catechism will offer criteria, motivations and modes of action to highlight the Christian presence in these critical situations.[50]

– Finally, the concrete ecclesial situation lived by a particular Church shall provide the context to which a catechism must make reference. Obviously one does not refer hereby to contin-

---

[47] Cf. CT 55c; MPD 7; DCG (1971) 34.
[48] Cf. CT 36-45.
[49] Local catechisms must give attention to the question and orientation of popular devotions (cf. EN 48; CT 54 and CCC 1674-1676). Equally they should be concerned with ecumenical dialogue (cf. CT 32-34; CCC 817-822) and with inter-religious dialogue (cf. EN 53; RM 55-57 and CCC 839-845).
[50] LC 72 distinguishes between "principles of reflection", "criteria of judgement" and "directives for action" which the Church offers in her social doctrine. A catechism should also distinguish these various levels.

gent situations, which are addressed by other magisterial documents, but to the more permanent situation which demands a more specific and appropriate evangelization.[51]

The creativity of local Churches in the elaboration of catechesis

134. Local Churches, in fulfilling the task of adapting, contextualizing and inculturating the Gospel message by means of catechisms, for different ages, situations and cultures must exercise a mature creativity. From the *depositum fidei* entrusted to the Church, local Churches select, structure and express, under the guidance of the Holy Spirit, their inner Master, all those elements which transmit the Gospel in its complete authenticity in a given situation.

For this difficult task, the *Catechism of the Catholic Church* is a "point of reference" to guarantee the unity of the faith. This present *General Catechetical Directory*, for its part, offers the basic criteria which govern the presentation of the Christian message.

135. In elaborating local catechisms it will be useful to remember the following points:

– it is a question, above all, of elaborating genuine catechisms, adapted and inculturated: in this sense, a distinction must be drawn between a catechism which adapts the Christian message to different ages, situations and cultures, and one which is a mere summary of the *Catechism of the Catholic Church* and serves as an introduction to its study. These are two different types.[52]

---

[51] It refers fundamentally to "the different socio-religious situations" faced by evangelization. These are examined in Part I, chap. I.

[52] On the distinction between local catechisms and syntheses of the *Catechism of the Catholic Church* see *"Orientamenti sulle sintesi del Catechismo della Chiesa Cattolica"*, of the Congregation for the Clergy and the Congregation for the Doctrine of the

– Local catechisms may be diocesan, regional or national in character.[53]

– with regard to the structuring of contents, different Episcopates publish catechisms of various structures and configurations; as has been said, the *Catechism of the Catholic Church* is proposed as a point of doctrinal reference, but, does not impose on the entire Church a determined structure on other catechisms: there are catechisms with a trinitarian structure; others are planned according to the stages of salvation; others again are organized along a biblical or theological theme (Covenant, Kingdom of God, etc.); some are structured around an aspect of the faith, while others again follow the liturgical year;

– with regard to the manner of expressing the Gospel message, the creativity of a catechism will have a bearing on its formulation and content,[54] evidently a catechism must be faithful to the deposit of faith in its method of expressing the doctrinal substance of the Christian message:"The individual churches—which are involved not only with men but also with their aspirations, their wealth and their poverty, with their manner of praying and living and their outlook on the world—must make their own the substance of the evangelical message. Without any sacrifice of the essential truths they must transpose this message

---

Faith. Among other things it notes: "syntheses of the *Catechism of the Catholic Church* can be erroneously understood to be substitutes for local catechisms even to the extent of discouraging these latter. However, they lack those adaptations to local situations particular to those who are catechized which is required of catechesis" (4).

[53] Cf. CIC 775 §§ 1-2.

[54] The question of language both in local catechisms and in catechetical activity is of supreme importance. Cf. CT 59.

into an idiom which will be understood by the people they serve and those who proclaim it"; [55]

The principle to be followed in this delicate task is indicated by the Second Vatican Council: "to seek out more efficient ways—provided the meaning and understanding of them is safeguarded—of presenting their teaching to modern man: for the deposit of faith is one thing, the manner of expressing it is quite another".[56]

The Catechism of the Catholic Church and local catechisms: the *symphony of faith*

136. The *Catechism of the Catholic Church* and local catechisms, each, with its own specific authority, naturally, form a unity. They are a concrete expression of the "unity of the same apostolic faith",[57] and, at the same time, of the rich diversity of formulations of the same faith. To those who contemplate this harmony, the *Catechism of the Catholic Church* and local catechisms together express a "symphony" of faith, a symphony inherent above all in the *Catechism of the Catholic Church* which has been drawn up with the collaboration of the entire Episcopate of the Catholic Church, a symphony harmonized with this and manifested in local catechisms. This symphony, this "chorus of voices of

[55] EN 63. In the delicate task of assimilation and translation mentioned in this text it is most important to bear in mind the observation of the Congregation for the Doctrine of the Faith and of the Congregation for the Clergy *"Orientamenti sulle sintesi del Catechismo della Chiesa Cattolica"*, 3: "The preparation of local catechisms, which have the *Catechism of the Catholic Church* as an authoritative and secure reference text (FD 4), remains an important objective for the various Episcopates. However, the foreseeable difficulties which can arise in such an undertaking can only be overcome by an adequate assimilation of the *Catechism of the Catholic Church*. Such assimilation even when it is accomplished over a long period of time prepares the theological, catechetical and linguistic ground for a work that really inculturates the contents of the Catechism".

[56] GS 62b.

[57] FD 4b.

the universal Church",[58] heard in the local catechisms and faithful to the *Catechism of the Catholic Church*, has a very important theological significance.

– It manifests the Catholicity of the Church: the cultural riches of the peoples is incorporated into the expression of the faith of the one Church.

– The *Catechism of the Catholic Church* and local catechisms make manifest to the ecclesial communion of which "the profession of the one faith" [59] is one of the visible links, "in which and formed out of which the one and unique visible Church of Christ exists".[60] The particular Churches, "parts of the one Church of Christ", form with the whole, the universal Church, "a peculiar relationship of mutual interiority" [61] The unity which thus exists between the *Catechism of the Catholic Church* and local catechisms makes visible this communion.

– The *Catechism of the Catholic Church* and local catechisms equally express, clearly, the reality of episcopal collegiality. The Bishops, each in his own diocese and together as a college, in communion with the Successor of Peter, have the greatest responsibility for catechesis in the Church.[62]

The *Catechism of the Catholic Church* and local catechisms, by their profound unity and rich diversity, are called to be a renewing leaven of catechesis in the Church. Contemplating them with her Catholic and universal gaze, the Church, that is, the entire community of the disciples of Christ, can say in truth: "This is our faith, this is the faith of the Church".

---

[58] RM 54b.
[59] CCC 815.
[60] LG 23a.
[61] CONGREGATION FOR THE DOCTRINE OF THE FAITH, Letter *Communionis notio*, n. 19 *l. c.* 843.
[62] Cf. CT 63b.

PART THREE

THE PEDAGOGY OF THE FAITH

The pedagogy of the faith

"Yet it was I who taught Ephraim to walk, I took them up in my arms; but they did not know that I healed them. I lead them with cords of compassion, with the bands of love, and I became to them as one who eases the yoke on their jaws, and I bent down to them and fed them" (Hos 11:3-4).

"And when he was alone, those who were about him with the twelve asked him concerning the parables. And he said to them, 'to you has been given the secret of the kingdom of God'". "But privately to his own disciples he explained everything" (Mk 4:10-11, 34).

"You have one Master, the Christ" (Mt 23:10)

137. Jesus gave careful attention to the formation of the disciples whom he sent out on mission. He presented himself to them as the only teacher and, at the same time, a patient and faithful friend.[1] He exercised real teaching "by means of his whole life".[2] He stimulated them with opportune questions.[3] He explained to them in a more profound manner what he had proclaimed to the crowds.[4] He introduced them to prayer.[5] He sent

[1] Cf. Jn 15:15; Mk 9:33-37; 10:41-45.
[2] Cf. CT 9.
[3] Cf. Mk 8:14-21; 8:27.
[4] Cf. Mk 4:34; Lk 12:41.
[5] Cf. Lk 11:1-2.

them out on a missionary apprenticeship.[6] He promised to them
the Spirit of his Father whom he sent to bring them to the complete truth,[7] and to sustain them in inevitable moments of difficulty.[8] Jesus Christ is "the Teacher who reveals God to Man
and Man to himself, the Teacher who saves, sanctifies and
guides. He is the Teacher who lives, who speaks, rouses, moves,
redresses, judges, forgives and walks with us day by day on the
path of history. He is also the Teacher who comes and will
come in glory".[9] In Jesus Christ, Lord and Teacher, the Church
finds transcendent grace, permanent inspiration and the convinc-
ing model for all communication of the faith.

The meaning and purpose of Part Three

138.   In the school of Jesus the Teacher, the catechist closely
joins his action as a responsible person with the mysterious action of the grace of God. Catechesis is thus an exercise in "the
original pedagogy of the faith".[10]

The transmission of the Gospel through the Church remains
before all else and forever the work of the Holy Spirit and has
in Revelation a fundamental witness and norm.

This will be found in chapter one. But the Holy Spirit works
through people who receive the mission to proclaim the Gospel
and whose competence and human experience form part of the
pedagogy of the faith.

Hence arises a series of questions which have been fully ex-
plored in the history of catechesis. These are concerned with cat-

---

[6] Cf. *Lk* 10:1-20.
[7] Cf. *Jn* 16:13.
[8] Cf. *Mt* 10:20; *Jn* 15:26; *Acts* 4:31.
[9] CT 9.
[10] CT 58.

echetical activity, its sources, its methods, those to whom it is addressed and the process of inculturation.

The second chapter is not intended to be an exhaustive examination of all of these aspects but it will deal with those points which today appear to have particular importance for the whole Church. It is the task of the various directories and other catechetical instruments of the particular Churches to respond to specific problems in an appropriate manner.

CHAPTER I

Pedagogy of God,
source and model of the pedagogy
of the faith [1]

Pedagogy of God

139. "God is treating you as sons; for what son is there whom his father does not discipline?" (*Heb* 12:7) The salvation of the person, which is the ultimate purpose of Revelation, is shown as a fruit of an original and efficacious "pedagogy of God" throughout history. Similar to human usage and according to the cultural categories of time, God in Scripture is seen as a merciful Father, teacher and sage.[2] He assumes the character of the person, the individual and the community according to the conditions in which they are found. He liberates the person from the bonds of evil and attracts him to himself by bonds of love. He causes the person to grow progressively and patiently towards the maturity of a free son, faithful and obedient to his word. To this end, as a creative and insightful teacher, God transforms events in the life of his people into lessons of wisdom,[3] adapting himself to the diverse ages and life situations. Thus he entrusts words of instruction and catechesis which are transmitted from generation to generation.[4] He admonishes with reward and punishment, trials and sufferings, which become a formative influ-

---

[1] DV 15; DCG (1971) 33; CT 58; ChL 61; CCC 53, 122, 684, 708, 1145, 1609, 1950, 1964.
[2] Cf. *Dt* 8:5; *Hos* 11:3-4; *Prov* 3:11-12.
[3] Cf. *Dt* 4:36-40; 11:2-7.
[4] Cf. *Ex* 12:25-27; *Dt* 6:4-8; 6:20-25; 3:12-13; *Jos* 4:20.

ence.[5] Truly, to help a person to encounter God, which is the
task of the catechist, means to emphasize above all the relationship that the person has with God so that he can make it his
own and allow himself to be guided by God.

The pedagogy of Christ

140. When the fullness of time had come God sent his Son,
Jesus Christ, to humanity. He brought to the world the supreme
gift of salvation by accomplishing his redemptive mission in a
manner which continued "the pedagogy of God", with the perfection found in the newness of his Person. In his words, signs
and works during his brief but intense life, the disciples had direct experience of the fundamental traits of the "pedagogy of Jesus", and recorded them in the Gospels: receiving others, especially the poor, the little ones and sinners, as persons loved and
sought out by God; the undiluted proclamation of the Kingdom
of God as the good news of the truth and of the consolation of
the Father; a kind of delicate and strong love which liberates
from evil and promotes life; a pressing invitation to a manner of
living sustained by faith in God, by hope in the Kingdom and
by charity to one's neighbour; the use of all the resources of in-
terpersonal communication, such as word, silence, metaphor, image, example, and many diverse signs as was the case with the
biblical prophets. Inviting his disciples to follow him unreservedly
and without regret,[6] Christ passed on to them his pedagogy of
faith as a full sharing in his actions and in his destiny.

---

[5] Cf. *Amos* 4:6; *Hos* 7:10; *Jer* 2:30; *Prov* 3:11-12; *Heb* 12:4-11; *Apoc* 3:19.
[6] Cf. *Mk* 8:34-38; *Mt* 8:18-22.

The pedagogy of the Church

141. From the her very beginnings the Church, which "in Christ, is in the nature of a Sacrament",[7] has lived her mission as a visible and actual continuation of the pedagogy of the Father and of the Son. She, "as our Mother is also the educator of our faith".[8]

These are the profound reasons for which the Christian community is in herself living catechesis. Thus she proclaims, celebrates, works, and remains always a vital, indispensable and primary *locus* of catechesis.

Throughout the centuries the Church has produced an incomparable treasure of pedagogy in the faith: above all the witness of saints and catechists; a variety of ways of life and original forms of religious communication such as the catechumenate, catechisms, itineraries of the Christian life; a precious patrimony of catechetical teaching of faith culture, of catechetical institutions and services. All of these aspects form part of the history of catechesis and, by right, enter into the memory of the community and the praxis of the catechist.

Divine pedagogy, action of the Holy Spirit in every Christian

142. *"Blessed is the the man whom thou dost chasten, O Lord, and whom thou dost teach out of thy law" (Ps* 94:12). In the school of the word of God, received in the Church, the disciple, thanks to the gift of the Holy Spirit sent by Christ, grows like his Teacher "in wisdom, stature, and in favour with God and men" (*Lk* 2,52). He is also assisted in developing in himself "the divine education" received by means of catechesis and by means

---

[7] LG 1.
[8] CCC 196; cf. GE 3c.

of knowledge and experience.[9] In this way, by knowing more about the mystery of salvation, by learning to adore God the Father, and "by living in the truth according to charity", the disciple seeks "to grow in all things towards him, who is the Head, Christ" (*Eph* 4:15). The pedagogy of God can be said to be completed when the disciple shall "become the perfect Man, fully mature with the fullness of Christ himself" (*Eph* 4:13). For this reason there cannot be teachers of the faith other than those who are convinced and faithful disciples of Christ and his Church.

Divine pedagogy and catechesis

143.   Catechesis, as communication of divine Revelation, is radically inspired by the pedagogy of God, as displayed in Christ and in the Church. Hence, it receives its constitutive characteristics and under the guidance of the Holy Spirit, it sets out a synthesis to encourage a true experience of faith, and thus a filial encounter with God. In this way, catechesis:

– is a pedagogy which serves and is included in the "dialogue of salvation" between God and the person, while giving due emphasis to the universal end of this salvation; with regard to God it underlines divine initiative, loving motivation, gratuity and respect for our liberty; with regard to man it highlights the dignity of the gift received and the demand to grow continually therein; [10]

– it accepts the principle of the progressiveness of Revelation, the transcendence and the mysterious nature of the word of God and also its adaptation to different persons and cultures;

---

[9] Cf. GE 4.
[10] Cf. PAUL VI, Ecyclical Letter, *Ecclesiam Suam* (6 August 1964), III: AAS 56 (1964), 637-659.

– it recognizes the centrality of Jesus Christ, the Word of God made man, who determines catechesis as "a pedagogy of the incarnation", and through whom the Gospel is to be proposed for the life and in the life of people;

– it values the community experience of faith, which is proper to the people of God, the Church;

– it is rooted in inter-personal relations and makes its own the process of dialogue;

– it conducts a pedagogy of signs, where words and deeds, teaching and experience are interlinked; [11]

– draws its power of truth and its constant task of bearing witness to it, since the love of God is the ultimate reason for his self-revelation, from the inexhaustible divine love, which is the Holy Spirit.[12]

Thus catechesis takes the form of a process or a journey of following the Christ of the Gospel in the Spirit towards the Father. It is undertaken to reach the maturity of the faith "given as Christ allotted it" (*Eph* 4,7) and according to the possibilities and the needs of everyone.

The original pedagogy of faith [13]

144.   Catechesis, which is therefore active pedagogy in the faith, in accomplishing its tasks, cannot allow itself to be inspired by ideological considerations or purely human interests.[14] It does not confuse the salvific action of God, which is pure grace, with the pedagogical action of man. Neither, however, does it oppose them and separate them. The wonderful dialogue that God un-

---

[11] Cf. DV 2.
[12] Cf. RM 15; CCC 24b-25; DCG (1971) 10.
[13] Cf. MPG 11; CT 58.
[14] Cf. CT 52.

dertakes with every person becomes its inspiration and norm. "Catechesis becomes an untiring echo" of this. It continually seeks dialogue with people in accordance with the directions offered by the Magisterium of the Church.[15] The precise objects which inspire its methodological choices are:

– to promote a progressive and coherent synthesis between full adherence of man to God (*fides qua*) and the content of the Christian message (*fides quae*);

– to develop all the dimensions of faith through which it conveys faith which is known, celebrated, lived and prayed; [16]

– to move the person to abandon himself "completely and freely to God": [17] intelligence, will, heart and memory;

– to help the person to discern the vocation to which the Lord calls him.

Catechesis therefore carries out a complete work of initiation, education and teaching.

Fidelity to God and to the person [18]

145.   Jesus Christ is the living and perfect relationship of God with man and of man with God. From him the pedagogy of the faith receives "a law which is fundamental for the whole of the Church's life", and therefore for catechesis: "the law of fidelity to God and of fidelity to man in a single, loving attitude".[19]

Genuine catechesis therefore is that catechesis which helps to perceive the action of God throughout the formative journey. It

---

[15] Cf. PAUL VI, Lett. enc. *Ecclesiam Suam, l.c.* 609-659.
[16] Cf. MPD 7-11; CCC 3; 13; DCG (1971) 36.
[17] DV 5.
[18] Cf. MPD 7; CT 55; DCD (1971) 4.
[19] CT 55.

encourages a climate of listening, of thanksgiving and of prayer.[20] It looks to the free response of persons and it promotes active participation among those to be catechized.

The "condescension" of God,[21] a school for the person

146.   God, wishing to speak to men as friends,[22] manifests in a special way his pedagogy by adapting what he has to say by solicitous providence for our earthly condition.[23] This implies for catechesis the never-ending task of finding a language capable of communicating the word of God and the creed of the Church, which is its development, in the various circumstances of those who hear it.[24] At the same time, it maintains the certainty that, by the grace of God, this can be done and that the Holy Spirit will give us the joy of doing it. Therefore pedagogical instructions adequate for catechesis are those which permit the communication of the whole word of God in the concrete existence of people.[25]

Evangelize by educating and educate by evangelizing[26]

147.   Being inspired by the pedagogy of faith, catechesis presents its service as a designated educative journey in that, on the one hand it assists the person to open himself to the religious dimension of life, while on the other, it proposes the Gospel to him. It does so in such a manner as to penetrate and transform

[20] Cf. DCG (1971) 10 and 22.
[21] DV 13; CCC 684.
[22] Cf. DV 2.
[23] Cf. DV 13.
[24] Cf. EN 63; CT 59.
[25] Cf. CT 31.
[26] Cf. GE 1-4; CT 58.

the processes of intelligence, conscience, liberty and action making of existence a gift after the example of Jesus Christ. Thus the catechist knows and avails of the contribution of the sciences of education, understood always in a Christian sense.

CHAPTER II

Elements of methodology

Diversity of methods in catechesis [1]

148. The Church, in transmitting the faith, does not have a particular method nor any single method. Rather, she discerns contemporary methods in the light of the pedagogy of God and uses with liberty "everything that is true, everything that is noble, everything that is good and pure, everything that we love and honour and everything that can be thought virtuous or worthy of praise" (*Phil* 4:8). In short, she assumes those methods which are not contrary to the Gospel and places them at its service. This is amply confirmed in the Church's history. Many charisms of service of the word have given rise to various methodological directions. Hence, the "variety of methods is a sign of life and richness" as well as a demonstration of respect for those to whom catechesis is addressed. Such variety is required by "the age and the intellectual development of Christians, their degree of ecclesial and spiritual maturity and many other personal circumstances".[2] Catechetical methodology has the simple objective of education in the faith. It avails of the pedagogical sciences and of communication, as applied to catechesis, while also taking account of the numerous and notable acquisitions of contemporary catechesis.

[1] CT 51.
[2] Cf. CT 51.

The content-method relationship in catechesis [3]

149. The principle of "fidelity to God and fidelity to man" leads to an avoidance of any opposition or artificial separation or presumed neutrality between method and content. It affirms, rather, their necessary correlation and interaction. The catechist recognizes that method is at the service of revelation and conversion [4] and that therefore it is necessary to make use of it. The catechist knows that the content of catechesis cannot be indifferently subjected to any method. It requires a process of transmission which is adequate to the nature of the message, to its sources and language, to the concrete circumstances of ecclesial communities as well as to the particular circumstances of the faithful to whom catechesis is addressed.

Because of its intrinsic importance both in tradition and in present day catechesis, mention must be made of the method of approaching the Bible, [5] of "documentary pedagogy", especially of the Creed, since catechesis is a transmission of the faith; [6] of the method of liturgical and ecclesial signs; and of methods proper to the mass media. A good catechetical method is a guarantee of fidelity to content.

Inductive and deductive method [7]

150. The communication of the faith in catechesis is an event of grace, realized in the encounter of the word of God with the experience of the person. It is expressed in sensible signs and is ultimately open to mystery. It can happen in diverse ways, not

---

[3] Cf. CT 31, 52, 59.
[4] Cf. CT 52.
[5] Cf. PONTIFICAL BIBLICAL COMMISSION, *The Interpretation of the Bible in the Church, l.c.*.
[6] MPD 9.
[7] DCG (1971), 72.

always completely known to us. With regard to the history of catechesis, there is common reference today to inductive method and deductive method. Inductive method consists of presenting facts (biblical events, liturgical acts, events in the Church's life as well as events from daily life) so as to discern the meaning these might have in divine Revelation. It is a method which has many advantages, because it conforms to the economy of Revelation. It corresponds to a profound urge of the human spirit to come to a knowledge of unintelligible things by means of visible things. It also conforms to the characteristics of knowledge of the faith, which is knowledge by means of signs. The inductive method does not exclude deductive method. Indeed it requires the deductive method which explains and describes facts by proceeding from their causes. The deductive synthesis, however, has full value, only when the inductive process is completed.[8]

151.   In reference to operative means, it has another sense: one is called "kerygmatic" *(descending)*, which begins with the proclamation of the message, expressed in the principle documents of the faith *(Bible, liturgy, doctrine...)* and applies it to life; the other is called "existential" *(ascending)*, which moves from human problems and conditions and enlightens them with the word of God. By themselves, these are legitimate approaches, if all factors at play have been duly observed; the mystery of grace and human data, the understanding of faith and the process of reason.

Human experience in catechesis [9]

152.   Experience has different functions in catechesis. For this reason, it must be continuously and duly evaluated.

---

[8] Cf. DCG (1971), 72.
[9] Cf. DCG (1971), 74; CT 22.

a) It arouses in man, interests, questions, hopes, anxieties, reflections and judgements which all converge to form a certain desire to transform his existence. It is a task of catechesis to make people more aware of their most basic experiences, to help them to judge in the light of the Gospel the questions and needs that spring from them, as well as to educate them in a new way of life. Thus, the person becomes capable of behaving in a responsible and active way before the gift of God.

b) Experience promotes the intelligibility of the Christian message. This corresponds well to the actions of Jesus. He used human experiences and situations to point to the eschatological and transcendent, as well as to show the attitude to be adopted before such realities. From this point of view, experience is a necessary medium for exploring and assimilating the truths which constitute the objective content of Revelation.

c) The above functions indicate that experience, assumed by faith, becomes in a certain manner, a *locus* for the manifestation and realization of salvation, where God, consistently with the pedagogy of the Incarnation, reaches man with his grace and saves him. The catechist must teach the person to read his own lived experience in this regard, so as to, accept the invitation of the Holy Spirit to conversion, to commitment, to hope, and to discover more and more in his life God's plan for him.

153.   Interpreting and illuminating experience with the data of faith is a constant task of catechetical pedagogy—even if with difficulty. It is a task that cannot be overlooked without falling into artificial juxtapositions or closed understandings of the truth. It is made possible, however, by a correct application of the cor-

relation and interaction between profound human experiences [10] and the revealed message. It is this which has amply borne witness to the proclamation of the prophets, the preaching of Christ, the teaching of the Apostles, which constitutes the basic normative criterion for every encounter of faith and human experience in the time of the Church.

Memorization in catechesis [11]

154. Catechetics forms part of that "memory" of the Church which vividly maintains the presence of the Lord among us.[12] Use of memory, therefore, forms a constitutive aspect of the pedagogy of the faith since the beginning of Christianity. To overcome the risk of a mechanical memorization, mnemonic learning should be harmoniously inserted into the different functions of learning, such as spontaneous reaction and reflection, moments of dialogue and of silence and the relationship between oral and written work.[13]

In particular, as objects of memorization, due consideration must be given to the principal formulae of the faith. These assure a more precise exposition of the faith and guarantee a valuable common doctrinal, cultural and linguistic patrimony. Secure possession of the language of the faith is an indispensable condition for living that same faith. Such formulae, however, should be proposed as syntheses after a process of explanation and should be faithful to the Christian message. To be numbered

---

[10] By this we mean those experiences linked with the "great questions" of life, reality and especially about the person: the existence of God, the destiny of the human person, the origin and end of history, the truth about good and evil, the meaning of suffering, of love and of the future...; cf. EN 53; CT 22 and 39.
[11] Cf. Part I, chap. III; DCG (1971) 73; CT 55.
[12] Cf. MPD 9.
[13] Cf. CT 55.

amongst them are some of the major formulae and texts of the Bible, of dogma, of the liturgy, as well as the commonly known prayers of Christian tradition: (Apostles' Creed, Our Father, Hail Mary...).[14]

"The blossoms—if we may call them that—of faith and piety do not grow in the desert places of a memoryless catechesis. What is essential is that texts that are memorized must at the same time be taken in and gradually understood in depth, in order to become a source of Christian life on the personal level and on the community level".[15]

155. Again, more importantly, the learning of the formulae of the faith and their profession must be understood in the traditional seed-bed or context of the *traditio* and the *redditio,* for which the handing on of the faith in catechesis (*traditio*) corresponds to the response of the subject during the catechetical journey and subsequently in life (*redditio*).[16]

This process encourages a greater participation in received truth. That personal response is correct and mature which fully respects the datum of faith and shows an understanding of the language used to express it (*biblical, liturgical, doctrinal*).

The role of the catechist [17]

156. No methodology, no matter how well tested, can dispense with the person of the catechist in every phase of the catechetical process. The charism given to him by the Spirit, a solid spirituality and transparent witness of life, constitutes the soul of ev-

---

[14] Cf. CCC 22.
[15] CT 55.
[16] Cf. Part I, chap. 3. *The baptismal Catechumenate: structure and progression.*
[17] DCG (1971), 71; cf. Part V, Chaps. 1 and 2.

ery method. Only his own human and Christian qualities guarantee a good use of texts and other work instruments.

The catechist is essentially a mediator. He facilitates communication between the people and the mystery of God, between subjects amongst themselves, as well as with the community. For this reason, his cultural vision, social condition and lifestyle must not be obstacles to the journey of faith. Rather, these help to create the most advantageous conditions for seeking out, welcoming and deepening the Christian message. He does not forget that belief is a fruit of grace and liberty. Thus, he ensures that his activities always draw support from faith in the Holy Spirit and from prayer. Finally, the personal relationship of the catechist with the subject is of crucial importance.

The activity and creativity of the catechized [18]

157. The active participation of all the catechized in their formative process is completely in harmony, not only with genuine human communication, but specifically with the economy of Revelation and salvation. Believers, indeed, in the ordinary state of Christian life, individually or in age groups, are called to respond to the gift of God through prayer, participation in the sacraments, the liturgy, ecclesial and social commitment, works of charity and promotion of human values, such as liberty, justice and peace and the protection of creation. In catechesis, therefore, subjects take on a commitment in activities of faith, hope and charity, to acquire the capacity and rectitude of judges, to strengthen their personal conversion, and to a Christian praxis in their lives. The same subjects, especially if adults, can contribute to catechesis, by pointing out the most effective ways of understanding and expressing the message such as: "learning while do-

[18] DCG (1971) 75.

ing", by employing research and dialogue, by exchanging challenging points of view.

Community, person and catechesis [19]

158.   Catechetical pedagogy will be effective to the extent that the Christian community becomes a point of concrete reference for the faith journey of individuals. This happens when the community is proposed as a source, *locus* and means of catechesis. Concretely, the community becomes a visible place of faith-witness. It provides for the formation of its members. It receives them as the family of God. It constitutes itself as the living and permanent environment for growth in the faith.[20]

Besides public and collective proclamation of the Gospel, person-to-person contact, after the example of Jesus and the Apostles, remains indispensable. In this way, personal conscience is more easily committed. The gift of the Holy Spirit comes to the subject from one living person to another. Thus, the power of persuasion becomes more effective.[21]

The importance of the group [22]

159.   Groups play an important function in the development processes of people. The same is true of catechesis, both for children where it fosters a rounded sociability, and for young people where groups are practically a vital necessity for personality formation. The same is true of adults where they promote a sense of dialogue and sharing as well as a sense of Christian co-responsibility. The catechist who participates in such groups and

[19] Cf. Part V Chap. 1.
[20] Cf. AG 14; DCG (1971), 35; CT 24.
[21] EN 46.
[22] DCG (1971), 76.

who evaluates and notes their dynamics recognizes and plays the primary specific role of participating in the name of the Church as an active witness to the Gospel, capable of sharing with others the fruits of his mature faith as well as stimulating intelligently the common search for faith. Apart from its didactic aspect, the Christian group is called to be an experience of community and a form of participation in ecclesial life. It finds its goal and fullest manifestation in the more extended Eucharistic community. Jesus says: "Where two or three are gathered in my name, there am I in their midst" (*Mt* 18:20).

Social communication [23]

160.   "The first areopagus of the modern age is the world of communication, which is unifying humanity... The means of social communication have become so important as to be for many the chief means of information and education, of guidance and inspiration in their behaviour as individuals, families and within society at large".[24] For this reason, in addition to the numerous traditional means in use, the media has become essential for evangelization and catechesis.[25] In fact, "the Church would feel herself guilty before God if she did not avail of those powerful instruments which human skill is constantly developing and perfecting... In them she finds in a new and more effective forum a platform or pulpit from which she can address the multitudes".[26]

In this respect, the following can be considered: television, radio, press, discs, tape recordings, video and audio cassettes,

---

[23] Cf. DCG (1971) 122-123; EN 45; CT 46; FC 76; ChL 44; RM 37; PONTIFICAL COUNCIL FOR SOCIAL COMMUNICATIONS, Instruction *Aetatis Novae* (22 Feb. 1992): AAS 84 (1992) pp. 447-468; EA 71; 122-124.

[24] RM 37.

[25] Cf. *Aetatis novae, l.c.,* n. 11.

[26] Cf. EN 45.

Compact Discs, as well as the entire range of audio-visual aids.[27]
All of these media offer a particular service and everybody will
have his own specific use for them. It is therefore necessary to
appreciate their importance and to respect their demands.[28] In
every well planned catechesis, such aids cannot be absent. Reciprocal assistance between the Churches, so as to defray the rather
high costs of acquiring and running such aids, is a true service
to the Gospel.

161.   Good use of the media requires of catechists a serious
commitment to knowledge, competence, training and up to date
use of them. But, above all, because of the strong influence of
the mass media and culture, it must be remembered that "it is
not enough to use the media simply to spread the Christian message and the Church's authentic teaching. It is also necessary to
integrate that message into the "new culture" created by modern
communications... with new languages, new techniques and a
new psychology".[29] Only by this, with the grace of God, can the
Gospel message have the capacity to penetrate the consciousness
of all and obtain a personal acceptance as well as a complete
personal commitment.[30]

162.   Those who work in the mass media, as well as those who
make use of them should be able to receive the grace of the
Gospel. This should cause catechists to consider particular
groups of people: media professionals to whom the Gospel can
be pointed out as a great horizon of truth, of responsibility and
of inspiration; families—who are so much exposed to the influence of the media—for their defence, but more so in view of a

---

[27] Cf. CT 46.
[28] Cf. DCG (1971), 122.
[29] RM 37.
[30] Cf. EN 45.

growing critical and educational capacity; [31] the younger generations, who are the users and creative subjects of mass media communications. All are reminded that "the use of these instruments by professionals in communication and their reception by the public demand both a work of education in a critical sense, animated by a passion for the truth, and a work of defence of liberty, respect for the dignity of individuals, and the elevation of the authentic culture of peoples".[32]

[31] Cf. FC 76.
[32] ChL 44.

PART FOUR

THOSE TO BE CATECHIZED

Those to be catechized

"I will give you as a light to the nations, that my salvation may reach to the ends of the earth" (Is 49:6).

"And he came to Nazareth, where he had been brought up; and he went to the synagogue, as his custom was, on the sabbath day. And he stood up to read; and there was given to him the book of the prophet Isaiah. He opened the book and found the place where it was written, 'The spirit of the Lord is upon me, because he has anointed me to preach good news to the poor. He has sent me to proclaim release to the captives and recovering of sight to the blind, to set at liberty those who are oppressed, to proclaim the acceptable year of the Lord'. And he closed the book, and gave it back to the attendant, and sat down; and the eyes of all in the synagogue were fixed on him. And he began to say to them: 'Today this scripture has been fulfilled in your hearing'" (Lk 4:16-21).

"The Kingdom is for all" [1]

163.   At the beginning of his ministry, Jesus proclaimed that he had been sent to announce a joyful message [2] to the poor, making it plain and confirming by his life that the Kingdom of God is for all men, beginning with those who are most disadvantaged. Indeed he made himself a *catechist* of the Kingdom of God for all categories of persons, great and small, rich and poor, healthy

[1] Cf. RM 15; EN 49-50; CT 35s; RM 14; 23.
[2] Cf. *Lk* 4:18.

and sick, near and far, Jews and pagans, men and women, righteous and sinners, rulers and subjects, individuals and groups. He is available to all. He is interested in the needs of every person, body and soul. He heals and forgives, corrects and encourages, with words and deeds.

Jesus concluded his earthly life by sending his disciples to do the same, to preach the Gospel to every creature on earth,[3] to "all nations" (*Mt* 28,19; *Lk* 24,47) "to the end of the earth", (*Acts* 1,8) for all time, "to the close of the age" (*Mt* 28,20).

164. Throughout her two-thousand-year history, the Church, continually prompted by the Holy Spirit, has accomplished the task of paying her obligation of evagelizing "both to Greeks, and to Barbarians, both to the wise and the foolish" (*Rm* 1,14) with an immense variety of experience in proclamation or catechesis. In this way the characteristics of a pedagogy of the faith have been articulated in which the universal openness of catechesis and its visible incarnation in the world of those to whom it is addressed, are clearly linked.

The meaning and purpose of Part Four

165. Attention to the diverse life situations of people [4] moves catechesis to employ many different approaches to meet them and to adapt the Christian message and the pedagogy of the faith to different needs.[5] The catechesis of initial faith is for catechumens and neophytes. Attention to the development in faith of the baptized gives rise to catechesis designed to deepen faith or indeed to recover faith, for those who need to discover that essential orientation again. When considering the physical and

---

[3] Cf. *Mk* 16:15.
[4] Cf. the General Introduction.
[5] Cf. DCG (1971), 77.

psychological development of those to be catechized, catechesis is developed according to age. In socio-cultural contexts, again, catechesis is developed within these categories.

166. Because it impossible to deal with every type of catechesis, this Part will restrict itself to a consideration of those aspects of catechesis which are of importance in any situation:

– general aspects of catechetical adaptation *(chapter 1)*;

– catechesis based on age *(chapter 2)*;

– catechesis for those who live in special circumstances *(chapter 3)*;

– catechesis in various contexts *(chapters 4 and 5)*.

The question of inculturation will also be approached in general terms, especially with reference to the content of the faith to persons and to cultural contexts. It is for particular Churches, in their national and regional catechetical directories, to give more specific directions with regard to concrete conditions and local needs.

CHAPTER I

Adaptation to those to be catechized: General aspects

The need and right of every believer to receive a valid catechesis [1]

167. All the baptized, because they are called by God to maturity of faith, need and have therefore a right to adequate catechesis. It is thus a primary responsibility of the Church to respond to this in a fitting and satisfactory manner. Hence it must be recalled that those to be evangelized are *"concrete* and historical persons",[2] rooted in a given situation and always influenced by pedagogical, social, cultural, and religious conditioning. They may or may not be aware of this.[3] In the catechetical process, the recipient must be an active subject, conscious and co-responsible, and not merely a silent and passive recipient.[4]

A community need and a community right [5]

168. In giving attention to the individual, it should not be overlooked that the recipient of catechesis is the whole Christian community and every person in it. If indeed it is from the whole life of the Church that catechesis draws its legitimacy and energy, it is also true that "her inner growth and correspondence with God's plan depend essentially on catechesis".[6]

---

[1] EN 49-50; CT 14; 35s.
[2] RH 13; cf. EN 31.
[3] Cf. RH 13-14; CCC 24.
[4] Cf. DCG (1971), 75.
[5] Cf. DCG (1971), 21.
[6] CT 13.

The adaptation of the Gospel both concerns and involves the community as a community.

Adaptation requires that the content of catechesis be a healthy and adequate food [7]

169. The "adaptation of the preaching of the revealed word must always remain a law for all evangelization". [8] There is an intrinsic theological motivation for this in the Incarnation. It corresponds to the elementary, pedagogical demands of healthy human communications and reflects the practice of the Church throughout the centuries. Such adaptation must be understood as a maternal action of the Church, who recognizes people as "the field of God" (*1 Cor* 3,9) not to be condemned but to be cultivated in hope. She sets out to meet each person, taking into serious account diversity of circumstances and cultures and maintains the unity of so many in the one saving Word. Thus the Gospel is transmitted as genuine, satisfying, healthy and adequate food. All particular initiatives must therefore be inspired by this criterion and the creativity and talent of the catechist must bow to it.

Adaptation takes account of diverse circumstances

170. Adaptation is realized in accordance with the diverse circumstances in which the word of God is transmitted. [9] These are determined by "differences of culture, age, spiritual maturity and social and ecclesial conditions amongst all of those to whom it is

---

[7] Cf. GS 44; EN 63; CT 31; CCC 24-25.
[8] GS 44. In this Part the terms *adaptation* and *inculturation* are used because they are employed in the Magisterium and for practical purposes. The first term mainly applies to attention given to persons while the second term is applied to cultural contexts.
[9] Cf. RM 33.

addressed".[10] Much careful attention shall be given to them. It shall be remembered that, in the plurality of situations, adaptation must always keep in mind the totality of the person and his essential unity, in accordance with the vision of the Church. For this reason catechesis does not stop with a consideration of the merely exterior elements of a given situation, but is always mindful of the interior world of the person, the truth of being human, "the first fundamental way of the Church".[11] In this manner a process of adaptation is determined which becomes the more suitable, the more the questions, aspirations and interior needs of the person are considered.

[10] CCC 24.
[11] RH 14.

CHAPTER II

Catechesis according to age

General observations

171. Catechesis based on different age groups is an essential task of the Christian community. On the one hand, faith contributes to the development of the person; on the other, every phase of life is open to the challenge of dechristianization and must above all be reinforced by ever new responses of Christian vocation.

Catechesis, therefore, is given by right on the basis of diverse and complementary age groups, on account of the needs and capacity of its recipients.[1]

For this reason it is necessary to pay attention to all the factors involved, whether anthropological-evolutionary or theological-pastoral, including also up to date scientific data and pedagogical methods prepared for different age groups. The various stages in the journey of faith must be prudently integrated, with care that successive phases of catechesis harmoniously complete catechesis received in childhood. Hence it is pedagogically useful to make reference to adult catechesis and, in that light, orientate catechesis for other times of life.

This chapter seeks to set out purely general elements, by way of example, and leaves further details to be worked out by the Catechetical Directories of particular Churches and of the Episcopal Conferences.

---

[1] Cf. CT 45.

THE CATECHESIS OF ADULTS [2]

Adults to whom catechesis is directed [3]

172. The discourse of faith with adults must take serious account of their experience, of their conditioning and of the challenges which they have encountered in life. Their questions of faith as well as their needs are many and varied.[4] Consequently, the following categories may be distinguished:

– adult Christians who consistently live their faith option and sincerely desire to deepen it;

– adults who have been baptized but who have not been sufficiently catechized, or have not brought to fulfilment the journey begun at Christian initiation, or who have fallen away from the faith, to such a degree that they may be called 'quasi catechumens'; [5]

– non-baptized adults, to whom the catechumenate truly and properly corresponds.[6]

Mention must also be made of those adults who come from Christian confessions which are not in full communion with the Catholic Church.

Elements and criteria proper to adult catechesis [7]

173. Adult catechesis concerns persons who have a right and a duty to bring to maturity the seed of faith sown in them by

---

[2] Cf. Part I, chap. II, nn. 142-144; DCG (1971), 20; 92-97; CT 43-44; COINCAT, *The catechesis of adults in the Christian community*, 1990.
[3] Cf. DCG (1971), 20; CT 19; 44; COINCAT, 10-18.
[4] Cf. COINCAT 10-18.
[5] CT 44.
[6] Cf. CT 19.
[7] Cf. DCG (1971), 92-94; COINCAT, 20-25; 26-30; 33-84.

God.[8] It is addressed to individuals who are charged to fulfill social responsibilities of various types and to those who are also prey to all kinds of changes and crises, sometimes profound. The faith of adults, therefore, must be continually enlightened, developed and protected, so that it may acquire that Christian wisdom which gives sense, unity, and hope to the many experiences of personal, social, and spiritual life. Adult catechesis requires the accurate identification of the typical characteristics of Christian adults. It must translate them into objectives and content, and determine certain constants of presentation. It must establish the most effective methodological approaches and choose formats and models. The role and identity of the catechists who work with adults and their formation—the people who are responsible for the catechesis of adults in the community—are vitally important.[9]

174.   Among the criteria which assure an authentic and effective adult catechesis, mention must be made of the following: [10]

– attention to those to whom it is addressed, to their condition as adult men and women, requires taking account of their problems and experiences, their spiritual and cultural resources, with full respect for their differences;

– attention to the lay condition of adults, on whom Baptism confers the task of "seeking the Kingdom of God by engaging in temporal affairs and directing them according to God's Will",[11] and whom it calls to holiness; [12]

– attention to the involvement of the community so that it may be a welcoming and supportive environment;

---

[8] Cf. *1 Cor* 13:11; *Eph* 4:13.
[9] Cf. COINCAT, 33-84.
[10] Cf. COINCAT, 26-30.
[11] LG 31; cf. EN 70; ChL 23.
[12] Cf. ChL 57-59.

– attention to ensure systematic pastoral care of adults, with which liturgical formation and the service of charity have been integrated.

General and particular tasks of adult catechesis [13]

175. So as to respond to the more profound needs of our time, adult catechesis must systematically propose the Christian faith in its entirety and in its authenticity, in accordance with the Church's understanding. It must give priority to the proclamation of salvation, drawing attention to the many difficulties, doubts, misunderstandings, prejudices and objections of today. It must introduce adults to a faith-filled reading of Sacred Scripture and the practice of prayer. A fundamental service to adult catechesis is given by the *Catechism of the Catholic Church* and by those adult catechisms based on it by the particular Churches. In particular, the tasks of adult catechesis are:

– *to promote formation and development of life in the Risen Christ* by adequate means: pedagogy of the sacraments, retreats, spiritual direction...

– *to educate toward a correct evaluation of the socio-cultural changes of our societies in the light of faith*: thus the Christian community is assisted in discerning true values in our civilization, as well as its dangers, and in adopting appropriate attitudes;

– *to clarify current religious and moral questions*, that is, those questions which are encountered by the men and women of our time: for example, public and private morality with regard to social questions and the education of future generations;

– *to clarify the relationship between temporal actions and ecclesial action*, by demonstrating mutual distinctions and implications

---

[13] Cf. DCG (1971), 97.

and thus due interaction; to this end, the social doctrine of the Church is an integral part of adult catechesis;

– *to develop the rational foundations of the faith*: that the right understanding of the faith and of the truths to be believed are in conformity with the demands of reason and the Gospel is always relevant; it is therefore necessary to promote effectively the pastoral aim of Christian thought and culture: this helps to overcome certain forms of fundamentalism as well as subjective and arbitrary interpretations;

– *to encourage adults to assume responsibility for the Church's mission and to be able to give Christian witness in society*:

The adult is assisted to discover, evaluate and activate what he has received by nature and grace, both in the Christian community and by living in human society; in this way, he will be able to overcome the dangers of standardization and of anonymity which are particularly dominant in some societies of today and which lead to loss of identity and lack of appreciation for the resources and qualities of the individual.

Particular forms of adult catechesis [14]

176. Certain situations and circumstances require special forms of catechesis:

– catechesis for the Christian initiation or catechumenate of adults: this has its own express form in the RCIA;

– traditional forms of catechesis of the people of God, duly adapted to the liturgical year or in the extraordinary form of missions;

[14] Cf. Part I, chap. 2; DCG (1971), 96.

– the on-going catechesis of those who have a task of formation in the community: catechists and those involved in the lay apostolate;

– catechesis for use in particularly significant events in life, such as Marriage, the Baptism of children and the other sacraments of initiation, at critical times during youth, in sickness etc.: in such circumstances, people are disposed more than ever to seek out the true meaning of life;

– is for special events and experiences, such as beginning work, military service, emigration etc.: these are changes which can give rise to interior enrichment or bewilderment and in which the need of God's saving word should be emphasized;

– catechesis for the Christian use of leisure time, especially during holidays and travel;

– catechesis for special events in the life of the Church and society.

These and many other forms of special catechesis, complement, but do not replace, the ongoing, systematic, catechetical courses which every ecclesial community must provide for all adults.

THE CATECHESIS OF INFANTS AND YOUNG CHILDREN [15]

The important context of infancy and childhood [16]

177. This age group, traditionally divided into early infancy or pre-school age and childhood, possesses, in the light of faith and reason, the grace of the beginnings of life, from which "valuable-possibilities exist, both for the building up of the Church and

---

[15] Cf. DCG (1971) 78-81; CT 36-37.
[16] DCG (1971) 78-79; ChL 47.

for the making of a more humane society".[17] As a child of God, in virtue of the gift of Baptism, the child is proclaimed by Christ to be a privileged member of the Kingdom of God.[18] For various reasons today, rather more than in the past, the child demands full respect and help in its spiritual and human growth. This is also true in catechesis which must always be made available to Christian children. Those who have given life to children and have enriched them with the gift of Baptism have the duty continually to nourish it.

Characteristics of catechesis for infants and children [19]

178. The catechesis of children is necessarily linked with their life situation and conditions. It is the work of various but complementary educational agents. Some factors of universal relevance may be mentioned:

    – Infancy and childhood, each understood according to its own peculiarities, are a time of primary socialization as well as of human and Christian education in the family, the school and the Church. These must then be understood as a decisive moment for subsequent stages of faith.

    – In accordance with accepted tradition, this is normally the time in which Christian initiation, inaugurated with Baptism, is completed. With the reception of the sacraments, the first organic formation of the child in the faith and his introduction into the life of the Church is possible.[20]

    – The catechetical process in infancy is eminently educational. It seeks to develop those human resources which provide an an-

---

[17] Cf. ChL 47.
[18] *Mk* 10:14.
[19] Cf. DCG (1971) 78-79; CT 37.
[20] Cf. CT 37.

thropological basis for the life of faith, a sense of trust, of freedom, of self-giving, of invocation and of joyful participation.
Central aspects of the formation of children are training in
prayer and introduction to Sacred Scripture.[21]

– Finally attention must be devoted to the importance of two
vital educational *loci*: the family and the school. In a certain
sense nothing replaces family catechesis, especially for its positive
and receptive environment, for the example of adults, and for its
first explicit experience and practice of the faith.

179.   Beginning school means, for the child, entering a society
wider than the family, with the possibility of greater development
of intellectual, affective and behavioural capacities. Often specific
religious instruction will be given in school. All this requires that
catechesis and catechists constantly co-operate with parents and
school teachers as suitable opportunities arise.[22] Pastors should
remember that, in helping parents and educators to fulfil their
mission well, it is the Church who is being built up. Moreover
this is an excellent occasion for adult catechesis.[23]

**Infants and children without religious support in the family or
who do not attend school** [24]

180.   There are indeed many gravely disadvantaged children
who lack adequate religious support in the family, either because
they have no true family, or because they do not attend school,
or because they are victims of dysfunctional social conditions or
other environmental factors. Many are not even baptized; others

---

[21] Cf. SACRED CONGREGATION FOR DIVINE WORSHIP, *Directory for Masses with
children*; AAS 66 (1974) pp. 30-46.
[22] Cf. DCG (1971) 79.
[23] Cf. DCG (1971) 78, 79.
[24] Cf. DCG (1971) 80-81; CT 42.

do not bring to completion the journey of initiation. It is the responsibility of the Christian community to address this situation by providing generous, competent and realistic aid, by seeking dialogue with the families, by proposing appropriate forms of education and by providing catechesis which is proportionate to the concrete possibilities and needs of these children.

CATECHESIS OF YOUNG PEOPLE [25]

Pre-adolescence, adolescence and young adulthood [26]

181. In general it is observed that the first victims of the spiritual and cultural crisis gripping the world [27] are the young. It is also true that any commitment to the betterment of society finds its hopes in them. This should stimulate the Church all the more to proclaim the Gospel to the world of youth with courage and creativity. In this respect experience suggests that it is useful in catechesis to distinguish between pre-adolescence, adolescence and young adulthood, attending to the results of scientific research in various countries. In developed regions the question of preadolescence is particularly significant: sufficient account is not taken of the difficulties, of the needs and of the human and spiritual resources of pre-adolescents, to the extent of defining them a *negated age-group*. Very often at this time the pre-adolescent, in receiving the sacrament of Confirmation, formally concludes the process of Christian initiation but from that moment virtually abandons completely the practice of the faith. This is a matter of serious concern which requires specific pastoral care, based on the formative resources of the journey of initiation itself. With regard to the other two categories, it is helpful to dis-

---

[25] Cf. DCG (1971) 82-91; EN 72; CT 38-42.
[26] Cf. DCG (1971) 83.
[27] Cf. General Introduction, 23-24.

tinguish between adolescence and young adulthood even though
it is difficult to define them strictly. They are understood together as the period of life which precedes the taking up of responsibilities proper to adults. Youth catechesis must be profoundly
revised and revitalized.

The importance of youth for society and the Church [28]

182.   The Church, while regarding young people as "hope", also
sees them as "a great challenge for the future of the Church" [29]
herself. The rapid and tumultuous socio-cultural change, increase
in numbers, self-affirmation for a consistent period before taking
up adult responsibilities, unemployment, in certain countries conditions of permanent under-development, the pressures of con-
sumer society—all contribute to make of youth a world in waiting, not infrequently a world of disenchantment, of boredom, of
angst and of marginalization. Alienation from the Church, or a
least diffidence in her regard, lurks in many as a fundamental attitude. Often this reflects lack of spiritual and moral support in
the family and weaknesses in the catechesis which they have received. On the other hand, many of them are driven by a strong
impetus to find meaning, solidarity, social commitment and even
religious experience.

183.   Some consequences for catechesis arise from this. The service of the faith notes above all the contrasts in the condition of
youth as found concretely in various regions and environments.
The heart of catechesis is the explicit proposal of Christ to the
young man in the Gospel; [30] it is a direct proposal to all young

---

[28] Cf. DCG (1971) 82; EN 72; MDP 3; CT 38-39; ChL 46; TMA 58.

[29] GE 2; ChL 46.

[30] Cf. *Mt* 19:16-22; cf. JOHN PAUL II, Apostolic Letter to Youth *Parati Semper* (31
March 1985): AAS 77 (1985), pp. 579-628.

people in terms appropriate to young people, and with considered understanding of their problems. In the Gospel young people in fact speak directly to Christ, who reveals to them their "singular richness" and calls them to an enterprise of personal and community growth, of decisive value for the fate of society and of the Church.[31] Therefore young people cannot be considered only objects of catechesis, but also active subjects and protagonists of evangelization and artisans of social renewal.[32]

Characteristics of catechesis for young people [33]

184. Given the extent of this task, the Catechetical Directories of particular Churches and national and regional Episcopal Conferences must, taking into account different contexts, determine more specifically suitable measures for these areas. Some general directions, however, may be indicated.

– The diversity of the religious situation should be kept in mind: there are young people who are not even baptized, others have not completed Christian initiation, others are in grave crises of faith, others are moving towards making a decision with regard to faith, others have already made such a decision and call for assistance.

– It should also be remembered that the most successful catechesis is that which is given in the context of the wider pastoral care of young people, especially when it addresses the problems affecting their lives. Hence, catechesis should be integrated with certain procedures, such as analysis of situations, attention to human sciences and education, the co-operation of the laity and of young people themselves.

---

[31] Cf. JOHN PAUL II, *"Parati semper"*, n. 3.
[32] ChL 46; DCG (1971) 89.
[33] DCG (1971) 84-89; CT 38-40.

– Well organized group action, membership of valid youth associations [34] and personal accompaniment of young people, which should also include spiritual direction as an important element, are useful approaches for effective catechesis.

185. Among the diverse forms of youth catechesis, provision should be made, in so far as circumstances permit, for the youth catechumenate during school years, catechesis for Christian initiation, catechesis on specific themes, as well as other kinds of occasional and informal meetings.

Generally youth catechesis should be proposed in new ways which are open to the sensibilities and problems of this age group. They should be of a theological, ethical, historical and social nature. In particular, due emphasis should be given to education in truth and liberty as understood by the Gospel, to the formation of conscience and to education for love. Emphasis should also be placed on vocational discernment, Christian involvement in society and on missionary responsibility in the world.[35] It must be emphasized, however, that frequently contemporary evangelization of young people must adopt a *missionary dimension* rather than a strictly *catechumenal* dimension. Indeed, the situation often demands that the apostolate amongst young people be an animation of a *missionary or humanitarian nature,* as a necessary first step to bringing to maturity those dispositions favourable to the strictly catechetical moment. Very often, in reality, it is useful to *intensify pre-catechumenal activity within the general educational process.* One of the difficulties to be addressed and resolved is the question of "language" (*mentality, sensibility,*

---

[34] DCG (1971) 87.

[35] Other important themes include: the relationship between faith and reason; the existence and meaning of God; the problem of evil; the Church; the objective moral order in relation to personal subjectivity; the encounter between man and woman; the social doctrine of the Church.

tastes, style, vocabulary) between young people and the Church (*catechesis, catechists*). A necessary "adaptation of catechesis to young people" is urged, in order to translate into their terms "the message of Jesus with patience and wisdom and without betrayal".[36]

CATECHESIS FOR THE AGED [37]

Old age, gift of God to the Church

186.   In many countries, the growing number of old people represents a new and specific pastoral challenge for the Church. Not infrequently the old are seen as passive objects and possibly even as an encumbrance. In the light of faith, however, they must be understood as a gift of God to the Church and to society, and must also be given adequate catechetical care. In catechesis, they have the same rights and duties as all Christians.

Attention must always be paid to the diversity of personal, family and social conditions. In particular, account must be taken of factors such as isolation and the risk of marginalization. The family has a primary function, since it is here that the proclamation of the faith can take place in an environment of acceptance and of love which best confirm the validity of the word. In any event, catechesis addressed to the aged will associate with the content of faith the caring presence of the catechist and of the community of believers. For this reason, it is most desirable that the aged participate fully in the catechetical journey of the community.

[36] CT 40.
[37] Cf. DCG (1971) 95; ChL 48.

Catechesis of fulfilment and hope

187.   Catechesis for the aged pays particular attention to certain aspects of their condition of faith. An aged person may have a rich and solid faith, in which case catechesis, in a certain sense, brings to fulfilment a journey of faith in an attitude of thanksgiving and hopeful expectation. Others live a faith weakened by poor Christian practice. In this case, catechesis becomes a moment of new light and religious experience. Sometimes people reach old age profoundly wounded in body and soul. In these circumstances, catechesis can help them to live their condition in an attitude of prayer, forgiveness and inner peace.

At any rate, the condition of the old calls for a catechesis of hope, which derives from the certainty of finally meeting God. It is always a personal benefit and an enrichment of the Christian community, when the old bear witness to a faith which grows even more resplendent as they gradually approach the great moment of meeting the Lord.

Wisdom and dialogue [38]

188.   The Bible presents us with the figure of the old man as the symbol of a person rich in wisdom and fear of God, and as a repository of an intense experience of life, which, in a certain sense, makes him a natural "catechist" in the community. He is a witness to a tradition of faith, a teacher of life, and a worker of charity. Catechesis values this grace. It helps the aged to discover the riches within themselves and to assume the role of catechists among children—for whom they are often valued grandparents—and for young people and adults. Thus a fundamental dialogue between the generations can be promoted both within the family and within the community.

[38] Cf. ChL 48.

CHAPTER III

Catechesis for special situations, mentalities and environments

Catechesis for the disabled and the handicapped [1]

189. Every Christian community considers those who suffer handicaps, physical or mental, as well as other forms of disability—especially children—as persons particularly beloved of the Lord. A growth in social and ecclesial consciousness, together with undeniable progress in specialized pedagogy, makes it possible for the family and other formative centres to provide adequate catechesis for these people, who, as baptized, have this right and, if non-baptized, because they are called to salvation. The love of the Father for the weakest of his children and the continuous presence of Jesus and His Spirit give assurance that every person, however limited, is capable of growth in holiness.

Education in the faith, which involves the family above all else, calls for personalized and adequate programmes. It should take into account the findings of pedagogical research. It is most effectively carried out in the context of the integral education of the person. On the other hand, the risk must be avoided of separating this specialized catechesis from the general pastoral care of the community. It is therefore necessary that the community be made aware of such catechesis and be involved in it. The particular demands of this catechesis require a special competence from catechists and render their service all the more deserving.

[1] Cf. DCG (1971) 91; CT 41.

The catechesis of the marginalized

190. The catechesis of the marginalized must be considered within the same perspective. It addresses itself to immigrants, refugees, nomads, travelling people, the chronically ill, drug addicts, prisoners. The solemn word of Jesus, which acknowledged, as done to him any good work done to "the least of the brethren" (*Mt* 25,40;45) guarantees the grace needed to work well in difficult environments. Permanent signs of the strength of catechesis are its capacity to identify different situations, to meet the needs and questions of everyone, to stress the value of generous and patient personal contact, to proceed with trust and realism, sometimes turning to indirect and occasional forms of catechesis. The Christian community fraternally supports those catechists who dedicate themselves to this service.

Catechesis for different groups

191. Catechesis, today, is confronted by subjects who, because of professional training or more broadly cultural formation, require special programmes. These include catechesis for workers, for professionals, for artists, for scientists and for university students. This is warmly recommended within the common journey of the Christian community. Clearly, all these sectors demand a competent approach and language adapted to those being catechized, while always maintaining fidelity to the message which catechesis transmits.[2]

Environmental catechesis

192. The service of the faith today takes careful note of the environment and human habitats. It is in these that the person

[2] Cf. CT 59.

lives his concrete existence. It is here that he is influenced and that he influences. Here too he exercises his responsibilities. Very broadly, two major environments must be mentioned: rural and urban. Both call for different forms of catechesis. The catechesis of country people will necessarily reflect needs experienced in the country. Such needs are often linked with poverty, sometimes with fear and superstition, but also rich in simplicity, trust in life, a sense of solidarity, faith in God and fidelity to religious traditions. Urban catechesis must take account of a variety of social conditions, sometimes so extreme as to extend from exclusive areas of prosperity to pockets of poverty and marginalization. Stress can dominate the rhythm of life. Mobility is easy. There are many temptations to escapism and irresponsibility. Oppressive anonymity and loneliness are widespread.

For both of these environments the service of the faith requires adequate planning, trained catechists, useful aids and familiarity with the resources of the mass-media.

CHAPTER IV

Catechesis in the socio-religious context

Catechesis in complex and pluralistic situations [1]

193. Many communities and individuals are called to live in a pluralistic and secularized world,[2] in which forms of unbelief and religious indifference may be encountered together with vibrant expressions of religious and cultural pluralism. In many individuals the search for certainty and for values appears strong. Spurious forms of religion, however, are also evident as well as dubious adherence to the faith. In the face of such diversity, some Christians are confused or lost. They become incapable of knowing how to confront situations or to judge the messages which they receive. They may abandon regular practice of the faith and end by living as though there were no God—often resorting to surrogate or pseudo-religions. Their faith is exposed to trials. When threatened it risks being extinguished altogether, unless it is constantly nourished and sustained.

194.   In these circumstances, a catechesis of evangelization becomes indispensable: a catechesis "which must be impregnated with the spirit of the Gospel and imparted in language adapted to the times and to the hearers".[3] Such catechesis seeks to educate Christians in a sense of their identity as baptized, as believers, as members of the Church, who are open to dialogue with the world. It reminds them of the fundamental elements of the faith. It stimulates a real process of conversion. For them, it

---

[1] Cf. EN 51-56; MPD 15.
[2] Cf. General Introduction.
[3] Cf. EN 54.

deepens the truth and the value of the Christian message in the
face of theoretical and practical objections. It helps them to discern the Gospel and to live it out in every-day life. It enables
them to give the reasons for the hope that is theirs.[4] It encourages them to exercise their missionary vocation by witness, dialogue and proclamation.

Catechesis and popular devotion [5]

195.   As a vital dimension in Catholic life, there exists in Christian communities, particular expressions of the search for God
and the religious life which are full of fervour and purity of intention, which can be called "popular piety". "For it does indicate a certain thirst for God such as only those who are simple
and poor in spirit can experience. It can arouse in them a capacity for self dedication and for the exercise of heroism when
there is a question of professing the faith. It gives men a keen
sensitivity by virtue of which they can appreciate the ineffable at-
tributes of God: his fatherly compassion, his providence, his
benevolence and loving presence. It can develop in the inmost
depths of man habits of virtue rarely to be found otherwise in
the same degree, such as patience, acceptance of the Cross in
daily life, detachment, openness to other men and a spirit of
ready service".[6] This is a rich yet vulnerable reality in which the
faith at its base may be in need of purification and consolida-
tion. A catechesis, therefore, is required which is of such religious richness as to be quick to appreciate its inherent nature
and its desirable qualities and zealous to direct it so that the
dangers arising out of its errors or fanaticism, superstition, syn-

---

[4] Cf. *1 Pet* 3:15.
[5] Cf. DCG (1971) 6; EN 48; CT 54.
[6] EN 48.

cretism, or religious ignorance may be avoided. "When it is wisely directed popular piety of this kind can make a constantly increasing contribution towards bringing the masses of our people into contact with God in Jesus Christ".[7]

196. Multiple forms of devotion to the Mother of God have developed in different circumstances of time and place, in response to popular sensibilities and cultural differences. Certain forms of Marian devotion however, because of long usage, require a renewed catechesis to restore to them elements that have become lost or obscured. By such catechesis the perennial value of Marian devotion can be emphasised, doctrinal elements gleaned from theological reflection and the Church's Magisterium assimilated. Catechesis on the Blessed Virgin Mary should always express clearly the intrinsic Trinitarian, Christological and ecclesiological aspects of mariology. In revising or drawing up materials for use in Marina peity account should be taken of biblical, liturgical, ecumenial and anthroplogical orientation. [8]

Catechesis in the context of ecumenism [9]

197. Every Christian community, by the mere fact of being what it is, is moved by the Spirit to recognize its ecumenical vocation in the circumstances in which it finds itself, by participating in ecumenical dialogue and initiatives to foster the unity of Christians. Catechesis, therefore, is always called to assume an

---

[7] EN 48.

[8] Cf. PAUL VI, Apostolic Exhortation *Marialis cultus* (2 February 1974), nn. 24, 25, 29, AAS 66 (1979), pp. 134-136, 141.

[9] Cf. DCG (1971) 27; MPG 15; EN 54; CT 32-34; PONTIFICAL COUNCIL FOR THE PROMOTION OF CHRISTIAN UNITY, *Directory for the application of principles and norms concerning Ecumenism,* 61 AAS 85 (1993) pp. 1063-1064; TMA 34; (cf. *Ut Unum sint* (25 May, 1995) n. 18 AAS 87 (1995), p. 932.

"ecumenical dimension" [10] everywhere. This is done, firstly, by an exposition of all of Revelation, of which the Catholic Church conserves the deposit, while respecting the hierarchy of truths.[11] In the second place, catechesis brings to the fore that unity of faith which exists between Christians and explains the divisions existing between them and the steps being taken to overcome them.[12] Catechesis also arouses and nourishes a true desire for unity, particularly with the love of Sacred Scripture. Finally, it prepares children, young people and adults to live in contact with brothers and sisters of other confessions, by having them cultivate both their own Catholic identity and respect for the faith of others.

198.   In the context of different Christian confessions, the Bishops may deem opportune or necessary specific ecumenical co-operation in the area of religious instruction. It is important, however, that Catholics are guaranteed, at the same time, a genuinely Catholic catechesis, by specific provisions and with all the more care.[13]

The teaching of religion in schools attended by Christians of diverse confessions can also have an ecumenical value when Christian doctrine is genuinely presented. This affords the opportunity for dialogue through which prejudice and ignorance can be overcome and a greater openness to better reciprocal understanding achieved.

---

[10] CT 32.
[11] Cf. UR 11.
[12] Cf. *Directory for the application of principles and norms concerning Ecumenism,* n. 190; *l.c.,* p. 1107.
[13] Cf. CT 33.

Catechesis in relation to Judaism

199. Special attention needs to be given to catechesis in relation to the Jewish religion.[14] Indeed "when she delves into her own mystery, the Church, the People of God in the New Covenant, discovers her links with the Jewish People, the first to hear the word of God".[15]

"Religious instruction, catechesis, and preaching should not form only towards objectivity, justice and tolerance but also in understanding and dialogue. Both of our traditions are too closely related to be able to ignore each other. It is necessary to encourage a reciprocal consciousness at all levels".[16] In particular, an objective of catechesis should be to overcome every form of anti-semitism.[17]

Catechesis in the context of other religions [18]

200. For the most part, Christians today live in multi-religious contexts; many, indeed, in a minority position. In this context, especially with relation to Islam, catechesis takes on a particular importance and is called to assume a delicate responsibility which is expressed in several duties. Above all, it deepens and strengthens, by means of appropriate adaptation or inculturation, the identity of believers—particularly where they constitute a minori-

---

[14] *Nostra Aetate,* SEGRETARIAT FOR CHRISTIAN UNITY, Commission for religious relations with Judaism, *Jews and Judaism in Catholic preaching and catechesis* 24 june 1985.

[15] CCC 839.

[16] *Jesus and Judaism in Catholic preaching and Catechesis,* n. VII.

[17] Cf. *Nostra Aetate,* 4.

[18] Cf. EN 53; MPD 15; ChL 35; RM 55-57; CCC 839-845; TMA 53; SACRED CONGREGATION FOR THE EVANGELIZATION OF PEOPLES - PONTIFICAL COUNCIL FOR INTER-RELIGIOUS DIALOGUE, *Dialogue and Proclamation* (19 May 1991): AAS 84 (1992), pp. 414-446; 1263.

ty—who find themselves in an obligatory encounter between the Gospel of Jesus Christ and the message of other religions. For this exchange, solid, fervent, Christian communities and well prepared, native catechists are indispensable. In the second place, catechesis assists in creating awareness of the presence of other religions. It necessarily facilitates Christians in discerning the elements in those religions which are contrary to the Christian message, but also educates them to accept the seeds of the Gospel (*semina Verbi*) which are found in them and which can sometimes constitute an authentic *preparation for the Gospel.*

In the third instance, catechesis promotes a lively missionary sense among believers. This is shown by clear witness to the faith, by an attitude of respect and mutual understanding, by dialogue and cooperation in defence of the rights of the person and of the poor and, where possible, with explicit proclamation of the Gospel.

Catechesis in relation to "new religious movements" [19]

201.   In a climate of cultural and religious relativism, and sometime because of the inappropriate conduct of Christians, a proliferation of "new religious movements" has occurred. These are sometimes called sects or cults but, because of the abundance of names and tendencies, are difficult to categorize in a comprehensive and precise framework. From available data, movements of Christian origin can be identified, while others derive from oriental religions, and others again appear to be connected with esoteric traditions. Their doctrines and their practices are of concern because they are alien to the content of the Christian faith.

[19] Report of the SECRETARIAT FOR CHRISTIAN UNITY, THE SECRETARIAT FOR NON-CHRISTIANS AND THE SECRETARIAT FOR NON-BELIEVERS AND THE PONTIFICAL COUNCIL FOR CULTURE *The Phenomenon of Sects or new religious movements: pastoral challenge, L'Osservatore Romano,* 7 May 1986.

It is therefore necessary to promote among Christians exposed to such risks "a commitment to evangelization and integral systematic catechesis which must be accompanied by a witness which translates these into life".[20] Thus it is necessary to overcome the danger of ignorance and prejudice, to assist the faithful in engaging correctly with the Scriptures, to awaken in them a lively experience of prayer, to defend them from error, to educate them in responsibility for the faith which they have received, confronting dangerous situations of loneliness, poverty and suffering with the love of the Gospel. Because of the religious yearning which these movements can express, they should be considered "a market place to be evangelized", in which some of the most pressing questions can find answers. "The Church has an immense spiritual patrimony to offer mankind, a heritage in Christ, who called himself 'the way, and the truth, and the life' (*Jn* 14:6)".[21]

---

[20] *The Phenomenon of Sects or new religious movements: pastoral challenge*, cit., n. 5. 4.
[21] RM 38.

CHAPTER V

Catechesis in the socio-cultural context [1]

Catechesis and contemporary culture [2]

202. "We can say of catechesis, as well as of evangelization in general, that it is called to bring the power of the Gospel into the very heart of culture and cultures".[3] The principles governing the adaptation and inculturation of catechesis have already been discussed.[4] It suffices to reaffirm that the catechetical discourse has as its necessary and eminent guide "the rule of faith", illuminated by the Magisterium of the Church and further investigated by theology. It must always be remembered that the history of catechesis, particularly in the patristic period, from several perspectives, is the history of the inculturation of the faith, and as such it merits careful study and meditation. It is, at the same time, an open-ended history which will continue to require long periods of ongoing assimilation of the Gospel. In this chapter, some methodological directions will be expounded concerning this task, as demanding as it is necessary, ever easy and open to the risks of syncretism and other misunderstandings. It can in-

---

[1] Cf. Part II, chap. 1; DCG (1971) 8; EN 20; CT 53; RM 52-54; JOHN PAUL II, Discourse to members of the International Council for catechesis, *L'Osservatore Romano,* of September 27, 1992; cf. CONGREGATION FOR DIVINE NORSHIP AND THE DISCIPLINE OF THE SACRAMENTS, *The Roman liturgy and Inculturation,* 1994; International Theological Commission, *Document on the faith and inculturation:* (25 Janury, 1985); AAS 87 (1995), pp. 288-319 *Commissio Theologica* on the Faith and Inculturation (3-8 October, 1988). Apostolic Exhortation *Ecclesia in Africa* (1995); cf. Discourses of John Paul II to the various Churches in his pastoral visits.
[2] Cf. EN 20; 63; CT 53; RM 52-54; CCC 172-175.
[3] CT 53.
[4] Cf. Part II, chap. 1.

deed be said on this subject, which is particularly important today, that there exists a need for greater systematic and universal
reflection on catechetical experience.

Duties of catechesis for inculturation of the faith [5]

203. These duties form an organic whole and are briefly expressed as follows:

– to know in depth the culture of persons and the extent of
its penetration into their lives;

– to recognize a cultural dimension in the Gospel itself, while
affirming, on the one hand, that this does not spring from some
human cultural *humus,* and recognizing, on the other, that the
Gospel cannot be isolated from the cultures in which it was initially inserted and in which it has found expression through the
centuries;

– to proclaim the profound change, the conversion, which the
Gospel, as a "transforming and regenerating" [6] force works in
culture;

– to witness to the transcendence and the non-exhaustion of
the Gospel with regard to culture, while at the same time discerning those seeds of the Gospel which may be present in culture;

– to promote a new expression of the Gospel in accordance
with evangelized culture, looking to a language of the faith which
is the common patrimony of the faithful and thus a fundamental
element of communion;

– To maintain integrally the content of the faith and esure
that the doctrinal formulations of tradition are explained and il-
lustrated, while taking into account the cultural and historical cir-

[5] CT 53.
[6] Cf. CT 53.

cumstaces of those being instructed, and to avoid defacing or falsifying the contents.

Methodological processes

204. Catechesis, while avoiding all manipulation of culture, is not limited to a mere juxtaposition of the Gospel with culture in some "decorative manner". Rather it proposes the Gospel "in a vital way, profoundly, by going to the very roots of culture and the cultures of mankind".[7] This defines a dynamic process consisting of various interactive elements: a listening in the culture of the people, to discern an echo (omen, invocation, sign) of the word of God; a discernment of what has an authentic Gospel value or is at least open to the Gospel; a purification of what bears the mark of sin (passions, structures of evil) or of human frailty; an impact on people through stimulating an attitude of radical conversion to God, of dialogue, and of patient interior maturation.

The need for and criteria of evaluation

205. In the evaluation phase, particularly in cases of initial attempts or experimentation, careful attention must always be given to ensuring that the catechetical process is not infiltrated by syncretistic elements. In instances where this happens, attempts at inculturation will prove dangerous and erroneous and must be corrected. In positive terms, a catechesis which inspires not only intellectual assimilation of the faith, but also touches the heart and transforms conduct is correct. Catechesis, thus, generates a dynamic life which is unified by the faith. It bridges the gap between belief and life, between the Christian message and the cultural context, and brings forth the fruits of true holiness.

[7] EN 20.

Those with responsibility for the processes of inculturation

206.   "Inculturation must involve the whole People of God, and not just a few experts, since the people reflect the authentic '*sensus fidei*' which must never be lost sight of. Inculturation needs to be guided and encouraged, but not forced, lest it give rise to negative reactions among Christians. It must be an expression of the community's life, one which must mature within the community itself and not be exclusively the result of erudite research".[8] The thrust to incarnate the Gospel which is the specific task of inculturation requires the co-operation in catechesis of all who live in the same cultural condition—clergy, pastoral workers (catechists) and laity.

Privileged forms and means

207.   Among the forms most apt to inculturate the faith, it is helpful to bear in mind catechesis of the young and adult catechesis on account of the possibilities which they offer of better correlating faith and life. Neither can inculturation be neglected in the Christian initiation of children precisely because of the important cultural implications of this process: acquiring new motivations in life, education of conscience, learning a biblical and sacramental language, knowledge of the historical density of Christianity.

A privileged means of this is liturgical catechesis with its richness of signs in expressing the Gospel message and its accessibility to so great a part of the people of God. The Sunday homily, the content of the Lectionary and the structure of the liturgical year should be valued afresh, along with other occasions of particularly significant catechesis (*marriages, funerals, visits to the sick,*

---

[8] RM 54.

feasts of patron saints etc.). The care of the family always remains central, since it is the primary agent of an incarnate transmission of the faith.

Catechesis also places special emphasis on multi-ethnic and multi-cultural situations in that it leads to a greater discovery and appreciation of the resources of diverse groups to receive and express the faith.

Language [9]

208. Inculturation of the faith, under certain aspects, is a linguistic task. This implies that catechesis respect and value the language proper to the message, especially biblical language, as well as the historical-traditional language of the Church *(creed, liturgy)* and doctrinal language *(dogmatic formulations).* It is also necessary for catechesis to enter into dialogue with forms and terms proper to the culture of those to whom it is addressed. Finally, catechesis must stimulate new expressions of the Gospel in the culture in which it has been planted. In the process of eculturating the Gospel, catechesis should not be afraid to use traditional formulae and the technical language of the faith, but it must express its meaning and demonstrate its existential importance. Similarly, it is also the duty of catechesis "to speak a language suited to today's children and young people in general and to other categories of people—the language of students, intellectuals and scientists; the language of the illiterate or of people of simple culture; the language of the handicapped, and so on".[10]

---

[9] Cf. CT 59.
[10] CT 59.

The media of communication

209. Intrinsically connected with the question of language is that of the means of communication. One of the most effective and pervasive means is the *mass media*. "The very evangelization of modern culture depends to a great extent on the influence of the media".[11]

While not repeating what has already been said of the *mass media* elsewhere,[12] some indications are proposed as useful in inculturation: a greater appreciation of the media for their specific communication quality, while realizing the importance of balancing the language of image and that of word; the safeguarding of the genuine religious meaning of selected forms of expression; the promotion of critical maturity among audiences, stimulating them to a deep, personal discernment of what has been received from the media; the production of catechetical aids congruent with this aim and the effective co-operation of all those engaged in pastoral initiatives.[13]

210. The catechism and, above all, the *Catechism of the Catholic Church* is central to the process of inculturation, and it must be used so as to evince a "vast range of services... which aim at inculturation, which, to be effective, must never cease to be true".[14]

The *Catechism of the Catholic Church* expressly calls for the preparation of appropriate local catechisms, incorporating those adaptations required by difference of culture, age, spirituality and in the social and ecclesial situations of those to whom catechesis is addressed.[15]

[11] RM 37.
[12] Cf. Part III, chap. 2.
[13] Cf. DCG (1971), 123.
[14] JOHN PAUL II, to the members of COINCAT *l.c.*
[15] CCC 24; JOHN PAUL II, *Fidei Depositum* 4.

Anthropological environments and cultural tendencies

211. The Gospel seeks a catechesis which is open, generous and courageous in reaching people where they live, especially in encountering those *nuclei* in which the most elementary and fundamental cultural exchanges take place, such as the family, the school, the work environment and free time.

It is important for catechesis to discern and penetrate these environments, as it is there that the major cultural tendencies have greater impact in creating and popularizing such models of life as urban life, migratory or tourist influxes, the world of youth and other socially relevant phenomena. Indeed "there are so many sectors to enlighten with the light of the Gospel",[16] especially those cultural areas denominated 'modern *areopagi*' like communications; civil campaigns for peace, development and liberation of peoples; the protection of creation; the defence of human rights, especially of minorities, women and children; scientific research and international relations.

Intervention in concrete situations

212. The process of inculturation operated by catechesis is continually called to confront many, different concrete situations. Here some of the more frequent and relevant are mentioned. In the first place, it is necessary to distinguish inculturation in countries of recent Christian origin, where the primary proclamation of the Gospel must yet be consolidated, from inculturation in countries of long Christian tradition which have need of new evangelization.

Account must also be taken of situations which are open to conflict and tension deriving from factors such as ethnic plural-

[16] Cf. RM 37.

ism, religious pluralism, differences of development which sometimes are strident; urban and extra-urban life-styles, dominant
thought-systems, which in some countries are strongly influenced
by massive secularization and by strong religiosity in others. Finally, inculturation seeks to respect the significant cultural tendencies of a particular country, represented in the various social
and professional strata, such as men and women of science and
culture, the world of workers, the youth, the marginalized, for-
eigners and the disabled. In more general terms, "the formation
of Christians will take the greatest account of local human culture, which contributes to formation itself, and will help to discern the value, whether implanted in tradition or proposed in
modern affairs. Attention should be paid to diverse cultures
which can exist in one and the same people or nation at the
same time".[17]

Tasks of the local Churches [18]

213.   Inculturation is a task for the particular churches and is
referred to by all areas of the Christian life. Precisely because of
the nature of inculturation which takes place in concrete and
specific circumstances, "a legitimate attention to the particular
Churches cannot but enrich the Church. It is indeed pressing
and indispensable".[19] To this end, and most opportunely, Episcopal Conferences, almost everywhere, are proposing Catechetical
Directories (and analogous instruments), catechisms and aids,
work-shops and centres of formation. In the light of what has
been expressed in the present Directory, an updating and revision of local directories becomes necessary. This should stimulate

---

[17] ChL 63.
[18] Cf. Part V, chap. 4.
[19] EN 63.

competition between centres of research, whilst availing of the experience of catechists and encouraging the participation of the people of God.

Guided initiatives

214. The importance of the matter, as well as, the indispensable phase of research and experimentation requires initiatives guided by legitimate Pastors. These include:

– promotion of widespread catechesis which serves to overcome ignorance and misinformation, the great obstacle of every attempt at inculturation: this permits that dialogue and direct involvement of persons who can best indicate effective ways of proclaiming the Gospel;

– carrying out pilot-schemes of inculturation of the faith within a programme established by the Church: the Catechumenate of adults according to the RCIA assumes a particularly influential role in this respect;

– if, in the same ecclesial area there are several linguistic or ethnic groups, it is always useful to provide for the translation of guides and directories into the various languages, promoting, by means of catechetical centres, an homogenous catechetical service for each group;

– setting up a dialogue of reciprocal learning and of communion between the Churches, and between these and the Holy See: this allows for the certification of experiences, criteria, programmes, tools and for a more valid and up to date inculturation.

PART FIVE

CATECHESIS
IN THE PARTICULAR CHURCH

Catechesis in the particular Church

"And he went up into the hills, and called to him those whom he desired; and they came to him. And he appointed twelve, to be with him, and to be sent out to preach and have authority to cast out demons" (Mk 3:13-15).

"Blessed are you, Simon Bar-Jonah! For flesh and blood has not revealed this to you, but my Father who is in heaven. And I tell you, you are Peter, and on this rock I will build my Church" (Mt 16:17-18).

The Church of Jerusalem moved by the Holy Spirit gave birth to the Churches: "The Church of God which is at Corinth" (1 Cor 1:2); "The Churches of Asia" (1 Cor 16:19); "The Churches of Christ in Judaea" (Gal 1:22); "The seven Churches: Ephesus, Smyrna, Pergamum, Thyatira, Sardis, Philadelphia, Laodicea" (cf. Apoc 2,1-3,22).

The meaning and purpose of Part Five

215.   From what has been said in the preceding parts concerning the nature of catechesis, its content, pedagogy, and those to whom it is addressed, there arises the nature of catechetical pastoral work, which is done in the particular Church. Part Five of this Directory presents its more important elements.

216.   The first chapter reflects upon the catechetical ministry and its agents. Catechesis is a shared but differentiated responsibility. Bishops, priests, deacons, religious and the lay faithful play their part, each according to their respective responsibilities and charisms.

The second chapter analyses catechists' formation, a decisive element in catechetical activity. If it is important that catechesis

224

be provided with valid catechetical material, yet more important is the preparation of suitable catechists. The third chapter studies the *loci* where catechesis is realized.

The fourth chapter studies the more organizational aspects of catechesis: the structures of responsibility, the co-ordination of catechesis and some tasks specific to catechetical service. The directives and suggestions offered in this section cannot find immediate and contemporary application in all parts of the Church. For those nations or regions in which catechetical activity has not yet had the means of reaching a sufficient level of development, these orientations and suggestions offer but a series of goals to be achieved gradually.

CHAPTER I

The ministry of catechesis in the particular Churches and its agents

The particular Church [1]

217. The proclamation, transmission and lived experience of the Gospel are realized in the particular Church [2] or Diocese.[3] The particular Church is constituted by the community of Christ's disciples,[4] who live incarnated in a definite socio-cultural space. Every particular Church "makes present the universal Church together with all of its essential elements". [5] In reality the universal Church, made fruitful by the Holy Spirit on the first Pentecost, "brings forth the particular Churches as children and is expressed in them".[6] The universal Church, as the Body of Christ, is thus made manifest as "a Body of Churches". [7]

---

[1] In Part Five as in the rest of the document the term *particular Church* refers to dioceses and there equiparates (CIC Canon 368). The term local Church refers to a group of particular Churches delineated in terms of Region or Nation or group of Nations united by special links. Cf. Part I, chap. III and Part II, chap. I. "The ecclesial nature of the Gospel message".

[2] As mentioned in LG 26a the term *Churches* in the NT is used to denote lawful groups of the faithful; see the biblical texts with which this part opens.

[3] Cf. CD 11.

[4] The particular Church is described before all else as *Populi Dei portio* or "a portion of the people of God".

[5] CONGREGATION FOR THE DOCTRINE OF THE FAITH, LETTERA *Communionis Noito,* 7 (AAS 85 -1993), 842.

[6] *Communionis Notio,* 9b.

[7] LG 23b refers to St Hilary of Poitiers In *Ps 14:3* (PL 9, 206) and St Gregory the Great *Moralia:* IV, 7, 12 (PL 75, 643 C).

218. The proclamation of the Gospel and the Eucharist are the two pillars on which is built and around which gathers the particular Church. Like the universal Church she also "exists for evangelization".[8] Catechesis is a basic evangelizing activity of every particular Church. By means of it the Diocese gives to all its members, and to all who come with a desire to give themselves to Jesus Christ, a formative process which permits knowledge, celebration, living and proclamation within a particular cultural horizon. In this way the confession of faith—the goal of catechesis—can be proclaimed by the disciples of Christ "in their own tongues".[9] As at Pentecost, so also today, the Church of Christ, "present and operative"[10] in the particular Churches, "speaks all languages",[11] since like a growing tree she extends her roots into all cultures.

The ministry of catechesis in the particular Church

219. In all the ministries and services which the particular Church performs to carry out its mission of evangelization, catechesis occupies a position of importance.[12] In this the following traits are underlined:

a) In the Diocese catechesis is a unique service[13] performed jointly by priests, deacons, religious and laity, in communion with the Bishop. The entire Christian community should feel responsi-

---

[8] EN 14.
[9] Cf. *Acts* 2:11.
[10] *Communionis Notio* 7.
[11] *Ibid.* 9b: *l.c.,* p. 843; cf. AG 4.
[12] The expression *ministry of catechesis* is used in CT 13.
[13] It is important to underline the nature of the one service which catechesis has in the particular Church. The subject of evangelizing activity is the particular Church. She proclaims and transmits the Gospel, which celebrates... The agents of catechesis "serve" this ministry and work "in the name of the Church." The theological, spiritual and pastoral implications of the ecclesial nature of catechesis are considerable.

ble for this service. Even if priests, deacons, religious and laity exercise catechesis in common, they do so in different ways, each according to his particular condition in the Church (*sacred ministers, consecrated persons and the Christian faithful*).[14] Through them all and their differing functions, the catechetical ministry hands on the word in a complete way and witnesses to the reality of the Church. Were one of these forms absent catechesis would lose something of its richness as well as part of its proper meaning;

b) On the other hand it is a fundamental ecclesial service, indispensable for the growth of the Church. It is not an action which can be realized in the community on a private basis or by purely personal initiative. The ministry of catechesis acts in the name of the Church by its participating in mission.

c) The catechetical ministry—among all ministries and ecclesial services—has a proper character which derives from the specific role of catechetical activity within the process of evangelization. The task of the catechist, as an educator in the faith, differs from that of other pastoral agents (*liturgical, charitable and social*) even if he or she always acts in coordination with them.

d) In order that the catechetical ministry in the Diocese be fruitful, it needs to involve other agents, not specifically catechists, who support and sustain catechetical activity by performing indispensable tasks such as: the formation of catechists, the production of catechetical material, reflection, organization and planning. These agents, together with catechists, are at the service of a single diocesan catechetical ministry even if all do not play the same roles or act on the same basis.

---

[14] CT 16: "Shared but differentiated responsibility". Cf. also note 54, as well as note 50 for a clarification of the term "ministry of the Word".

The Christian community and responsibility for catechesis

220.   Catechesis is a responsibility of the entire Christian community. Christian initiation, indeed, "should not be the work of catechists and priests alone, but of the whole community of the faithful".[15] Continuing education in the faith is a question which concerns the whole community; catechesis, therefore, is an educational activity which arises from the particular responsibility of every member of the community, in a rich context of relationships, so that catechumens and those being catechized are actively incorporated into the life of the community. The Christian community follows the development of catechetical processes, for children, young people and adults, as a duty that involves and binds it directly.[16] Again, at the end of the catechetical process, it is the Christian community that welcomes the catechized in a fraternal environment, "in which they will be able to live in the fullest way what they have learned".[17]

221.   The Christian community not only gives much to those who are being catechized but also receives much from them. New converts, especially adolescents and adults, in adhering to Jesus Christ, bring to the community which receives them new religious and human wealth. Thus the community grows and develops. Catechesis not only brings to maturity the faith of those being catechized but also brings the community itself to maturity.

        Yet, while the entire Christian community is responsible for Christian catechesis and all of it members bear witness to the

---

[15] AG 14. In this sense CT 16 says: "Catechesis always has been, and always will be a work for which the whole Church must feel responsible and must wish to be responsible." Cf. also 1977 Synod; MPG 12; RCIA 12; CIC 774 § 1.

[16] Catechesis must be supported by the *witness* of the ecclesial community, DCG (1971) 35; cf. part IV, chapter 2.

[17] CT 24.

faith, only some receive the ecclesial mandate to be catechists. Together with the primordial mission which parents have in relation to their children, the Church confers the delicate task of organically transmitting the faith within the community on particular, specifically called members of the people of God.[18]

The Bishop has primary responsibility for catechesis in the particular Church

222.   The Second Vatican Council gave much importance to the proclamation and transmission of the Gospel in the episcopal ministry. "Among the principal duties of Bishops, that of preaching the Gospel excels".[19] In carrying out this task, Bishops are, above all, "heralds of the faith",[20] seeking new disciples for Jesus Christ, and "authentic teachers",[21] transmitting the faith to be professed and lived to those entrusted to their care. Missionary proclamation and catechesis are two closely united aspects of the prophetic ministry of Bishops. To perform this duty Bishops receive "the charism of truth".[22] The Bishops are "beyond all others the ones primarily responsible for catechesis and catechists par excellence".[23] In the Church's history the preponderant role of great and saintly Bishops is evident. Their writings and initiatives mark the richest period of the catechumenate. They regard-

---

[18] "Besides this apostolate, which belongs to absolutely every Christian, the laity can be called in different ways to more immediate co-operation in the apostolate of the hierarchy, like those men and women who helped the apostle Paul in the Gospel, labouring much in the Lord" (LG 33). This conciliar doctrine is adopted by CIC 228 and 759.
[19] LG 25; cf. CD 12a; EN 68c.
[20] LG 25.
[21] Ibid.
[22] DV 8.
[23] CT 63b.

ed catechesis as one of the most fundamental tasks of their ministry.[24]

223. This concern for catechetical activity will lead the Bishop to assume "the overall direction of catechesis" [25] in the particular Church, which implies among other things:

– that he ensure *effective priority* for an active and fruitful catechesis in his Church "putting into operation the necessary personnel, means and equipment, and also financial resources"; [26]

– that he exercise solicitude for catechesis by direct intervention in the transmission of the Gospel to the faithful, and that he be vigilant with regard to the authencity of the faith as well as with regard to the quality of texts and instruments being used in catechesis; [27]

– "that he bring about and maintain... *a real passion for catechesis*, a passion embodied in a pertinent and effective organization",[28] out of a profound conviction of the importance of catechesis for the Christian life of the diocese;

– that he ensure *"that catechists are adequately prepared for their task*, being well instructed in the doctrine of the Church and possessing both a practical and theoretical knowledge of the laws of psychology and educational method"; [29]

– that he establish an *articulated, coherent and global programme* in the Diocese in order to respond to the true needs of the faithful: it should be integrated into the diocesan pastoral

---

[24] Cf. CT 12a.
[25] CT 63c.
[26] CT 63c; CIC 775 § 1.
[27] Cf. CT 63c; CIC 823 § 1.
[28] CT 63c.
[29] CD 14b; CIC 780.

plan and co-ordinated with the programmes of the Episcopal Conference.

Priests, pastors and educators of the Christian community

224.   The function proper to the presbyterate in the catechetical task arises from the sacrament of Holy Orders which they have received. "Through that sacrament priests, by the anointing of the Holy Spirit, are signed with a special character and so are configured to Christ the priest, in such a way that they are able to act in the person of Christ the head".[30] In virtue of this onto-logical configuration to Christ, the ministry of the priest is a ser-vice which forms the Christian community and co-ordinates and strengthens other charisms and services. In catechesis the sacra-ment of Holy Orders constitutes priests as "educators of the faith".[31] They work, therefore, to see that the faithful are proper-ly formed and reach true Christian maturity.[32] Conscious, on the other hand, that their "ministerial Priesthood" [33] is at the service of "the common Priesthood of the faithful",[34] priests foster the vocation and work of catechists and assist them in carrying out a function which springs from Baptism and is exercised in virtue of a mission entrusted to them by the Church. Thus priests put into effect the request which the Second Vatican Council made of them: "to recognize and promote the dignity of the laity and their specific role in the Church's mission".[35]

[30] Cf. PO 8; 6; 12a; JOHN PAUL II, Post synodal exhortation *Pastores dabo vobis* (25 March 1992), n. 12 *l.c.* 675-677.
[31] PO 6b.
[32] Cf. CIC 773.
[33] LG 10.
[34] LG 10. Concerning the "two ways of participating in the single priesthood of Jesus Christ", cf. CCC 1546-1547.
[35] PO 9b.

225. The catechetical tasks proper to the presbyterate and particularly to parish priests are: [36]

– to foster a sense of *common responsibility* for catechesis in the Christian community, a task which involves all, and a recognition and appreciation for catechists and their mission;

– to care for the *basic orientation of catechesis* and its planning by giving emphasis to active participation of catechists and by insisting that catechesis be "well structured and oriented"; [37]

– to promote and to discern *vocations* to the service of catechesis and, as catechist of catechists, attend to their formation by giving the greatest attention to this duty;

– to integrate catechetical activity into his programme of *community evangelization*; and foster the link between catechesis sacramets and the liturgy;

– to secure the bonds between the catechesis of his community and the *diocesan pastoral programme* by helping catechists become active co-operators in a common diocesan programme.

Experience bears out that the quality of catechesis in a community depends very largely on the presence and activity of the priest.

---

[36] Cf. CIC 776-777.
[37] CT 64. With respect to this basic orientation which priests must collaborate in giving to catechesis, the Second Vatican Council indicates two basic requirements: "their role is to teach not their own wisdom but the word of God", (PO 4) and "to expound the word of God not merely in a general and abstract way but by an application of the eternal truth of the Gospel to the concrete circumstances of life" (*ibid.*).

Parents, primary educators of their children [38]

226.   The witness of Christian life given by parents in the family comes to children with tenderness and parental respect. Children thus perceive and joyously live the closeness of God and of Jesus made manifest by their parents in such a way that this first Christian experience frequently leaves decisive traces which last throughout life. This childhood religious awakening which takes place in the family is irreplaceable.[39] It is consolidated when, on the occasion of certain family events and festivities, "care is taken to explain in the home the Christian or religious content of these events".[40] It is deepened all the more when parents comment on the more methodical catechesis which their children later receive in the Christian community and help them to appropriate it. Indeed, "family catechesis precedes...accompanies and enriches all forms of catechesis".[41]

227.   Parents receive in the sacrament of Matrimony "the grace and the ministry of the Christian education of their children",[42] to whom they transmit and bear witness to human and religious values. This educational activity which is both human and religious is "a true ministry",[43] through which the Gospel is transmitted and radiated so that family life is transformed into a journey of faith and the school of Christian life. As the children grow, exchange of faith becomes mutual and "in a catechetical

---

[38] Cf. chap. 3 of this Part, *The family as an environment or means of growth in the faith,* where the characteristics of family catechesis are analysed; here, more consideration is given to parents as agents of catechesis. Cf. CIC 226 § 2; 774 § 2.
[39] CT 68.
[40] *Ibid.*
[41] *Ibid.*
[42] Cf. ChL 62; cf. FC 38.
[43] FC 38.

dialogue of this sort, each individual both receives and gives".[44] It is for this reason that the Christian community must give very special attention to parents. By means of personal contact, meetings, courses and also adult catechesis directed toward parents, the Christian community must help them assume their responsibility—which is particularly delicate today—of educating their children in the faith. This is especially pressing in those areas where civil legislation does not permit or makes difficult freedom of education in the faith.[45] In this case "the domestic Church" [46] is virtually the only environment in which children and young people can receive authentic catechesis.

The role of religious in catechesis

228.   In a special way the Church calls those in consecrated life to catechetical activity and wishes that "religious communities dedicate as much as possible of what ability and means that they have to the specific work of catechesis".[47] The particular contribution to catechesis of religious and of members of societies of apostolic life derives from their specific condition. The profession of the evangelical counsels, which characterizes the religious life, constitutes a gift to the whole Christian community. In diocesan catechetical activity their original and particular contribution can never be substituted for by priests or by laity. This original contribution is born of public witness to their consecration, which makes them a living sign of the reality of the Kingdom: "it is the profession of these counsels, within a permanent state of life recognized by the Church, that characterizes the life consecrated

---

[44] CT 68; cf. EN 71b.
[45] Cf. CT 68.
[46] LG 11; FC 36b.
[47] CT 65; cf. CIC 778.

to God".[48] Although evangelical values must be lived by every Christian, those in consecrated life "incarnate the Church in her desire to abandon herself to the radicalism of the beatitudes".[49] The witness of religious united to the witness of the laity shows forth the one face of the Church which is a sign of the Kingdom of God.[50]

229. "Many religious institutes for men and women came into being for the purpose of giving Christian education to children and young people, especially the most abandoned".[51] That same charism of the founders is such that many religious collaborate today in diocesan adult catechesis. Throughout history many men and women religious "have been committed to the Church's catechetical activity".[52] The founding charisms [53] are not a marginal consideration when religious assume catechetical tasks. While maintaining intact the proper character of catechesis, the charisms of the various religious communities express this common task but with their own proper emphases, often of great religious, social and pedagogical depth. The history of catechesis demonstrates the vitality which these charisms have brought to the Church's educational activity.

Lay catechists

230. The catechetical activity of the laity also has a proper character which is due to their condition in the Church: "their

---

[48] CCC 915; cf. LG 44.
[49] EN 69; cf. VC 33.
[50] Cf. VC 31 concerning *"the relationship between the diverse states of life of the Christian"*; cf. CCC 932.
[51] CT 65; cf. RM 69.
[52] CT 65.
[53] Cf. *1 Cor* 12:4; cf. LG 12b.

secular character is proper and peculiar to the laity".[54] The laity
engage in catechesis on the basis of their insertion in the world,
sharing all the demands of humanity and bringing to the transmission of the Gospel specific sensitivity and nuances: "this
evangelization, that is, the proclamation of Christ by word and
the testimony of life, acquires a specific property and peculiar efficacy because it is accomplished in the ordinary circumstances of
the world".[55] Indeed by sharing the same form of life as those
whom they catechize, lay catechists have a special sensitivity for
incarnating the Gospel in the concrete life of men and women.
Catechumens and those receiving catechesis can find in them a
Christian model for their future as believers.

231.   The vocation of the laity to catechesis springs from the
sacrament of Baptism. It is strengthened by the sacrament of
Confirmation. Through the sacraments of Baptism and Confirmation they participate in the "priestly, prophetic and kingly ministry of Christ".[56] In addition to the common vocation of the
apostolate, some lay people feel called interiorly by God to assume the service of catechist. The Church awakens and discerns
this divine vocation and confers the mission to catechize. The
Lord Jesus invites men and women, in a special way, to follow
him, teacher and formator of disciples. This personal call of Jesus Christ and its relationship to him are the true moving forces
of catechetical activity. "From this loving knowledge of Christ
springs the desire to proclaim him, to 'evangelize,' and to lead
others to the 'Yes' of faith in Jesus Christ".[57] To feel called to
be a catechist and to receive this mission from the Church ac-

[54] LG 31. ChL 15 contains a detailed analysis of the 'secular character' of the lay faithful.
[55] LG 35.
[56] AA 2b. cf. Rituale Romanum, Ordo Baptisimi Parvulorum, n. 62, Editio Typica,
Typis Polyglottis Vaticanis 1969; RCIA 224.
[57] CCC 429.

quires different levels of dedication inaccordance with the particular characteristics of individuals. At times the catechist can collaborate in the service of catechesis over a limited period or purely on an occasional basis, but it is always a valuable service and a worthy collaboration. The importance of the ministry of catechesis, however, would suggest that there should be in a Diocese a certain number of religious and laity publicly recognized and permanently dedicated to catechesis who, in communion with the priests and the Bishop, give to this diocesan service that ecclesial form which is proper to it.[58]

Various types of catechists particularly necessary today

232.   The figure of the catechist in the Church, has different modes, just as, the needs of catechesis are varied.

– "The *catechists in missionary countries"*,[59] to whom this title is applied in a special way: "Churches that are flourishing today would not have been built up without them".[60] There are those who have the "specific responsibility for catechesis"; [61] and there are those who collaborate in various forms of apostolate.[62]

– In some Churches of ancient Christian tradition but where there is a shortage of clergy, there is need for catechists in some way analogous to those of missionary countries. This requires confronting urgent needs: the community animation of *small rural*

---

[58] The *Code of Canon Law* establishes that ecclesiastical authority may officially entrust an office or an ecclesial service to the laity, prescinding from the fact that this service is or is not a formally instituted *non-ordained ministry*: "lay people, who are found to be suitable, are capable of being admitted by the sacred pastors to those ecclesiastical offices and functions which, in accordance with the provisions of law, they can discharge" (CIC 228 § 1); cf. EN 73; ChL 23.

[59] CT 66b; cf. GCM.

[60] CT 66b.

[61] GCM 4.

[62] *Ibid.*

populations deprived of the constant presence of a priest, the helpfulness of a missionary presence "in areas of *large cities*".[63]

– In countries of Christian tradition which require a "new evangelization" [64] the *catechist for young people* and the *catechist for adults* become indispensable, in promoting the process of initiatory catechesis. The catechists must provide for continuing catechesis. In such tasks the role of the priest is equally fundamental.

– *The catechist for children and adolescents* continues to be indispensable. This catechist has the delicate mission of giving "the first notions of catechism and preparation for the sacrament of Penance, for First Communion and Confirmation".[65] This responsibility is all the more pressing today if children and adolescents "do not receive adequate religious formation within the family".[66]

– A catechist who must also be formed is the *catechist for pre-sacramental encounter*,[67] for adults on occasions such as the Baptism or the First Holy Communion of their children or the celebration of the sacrament of Matrimony. It is a specific and original task comprising the welcome of the faithful, of primary proclamation to them and of accompanying them on the journey of faith.

– Other catechists urgently needed in delicate human situations include catechists for the old [68] who need a presentation of the Gospel adapted to their condition; for handicapped or disabled people who require a special pedagogy,[69] in addition to

---

[63] CT 45; cf. RM 37, a/b, par. 2.
[64] RM 33.
[65] CT 66a.
[66] *Ibid.;* cf. CT 42.
[67] Cf. DCG (1971) 96.
[68] Cf. CT 45; cf. DCG (1971) 95.
[69] Cf. DCG (1971) 91; cf. CT 41.

their total integration into the community; for *migrants* and those *marginalized* by the evolution of modern society.[70]

– Other types of catechists may also be advisable. Every local Church, by analysing her own cultural and religious situation, will discover her own needs and will realistically foster those kinds of catechists which she needs. The organization and orientation of the formation of catechists is a fundamental responsibility.

[70] CT 45a.

CHAPTER II

Formation for the service of catechesis

Pastoral care of catechists in a Particular Church

233. To ensure the working of the catechetical ministry in a local Church, it is fundamental to have adequate pastoral care of catechists. Several elements must be kept in mind in this respect. Indeed efforts must be made:

– to encourage in parishes and Christian communities *vocations* for catechesis. Today, because the needs of catechesis are so varied, it is necessary to promote different kinds of catechists. "There is therefore a need for specialised catechists".[1] In this respect selection criteria must be established;

– to try to provide a certain number of *full time catechists* so that these can devote their time intensely and in a more stable way to catechesis,[2] in addition to fostering *part-time catechists* who are likely to be more numerous in the ordinary course of events;

– to organize a *more balanced distribution of catechists*, among the various groups who require catechesis. Awareness of the needs of adult catechesis and catechesis for young people, for example, can help to establish a greater balance in relation to the number of catechists who work with children and adolescents.

---

[1] GMC, 5.

[2] In missionary territories (CT 66) the Second Vatican Council distinguishes two types of catechist: full time catechists and auxiliary catechists (cf. AG 17). This distinction is taken up in the *Guide for Catechists* 4, which refers to them as full-time catechists and part-time catechists.

– to foster *animators of catechetical activity* with responsibility at diocesan level, in regions and in parishes.[3]

– to organize adequately the *formation of catechists,* both in relation to basic training and continuing formation.

– to attend to the *personal and spiritual needs of catechists as well as to the group of catechists as such.* This activity is principally and fundamentally the responsibility of the priests of the respective Christian communities.

– to *co-ordinate catechists* with other pastoral workers in Christian communities, so that the entire work of evangelization will be consistent and to ensure that catechists will not be isolated from or unrelated to the life of the community.

Importance of the formation of Catechists

234. All of these tasks are born of the conviction that the quality of any form of pastoral activity is placed at risk if it does not rely on truly competent and trained personnel. The instruments provided for catechesis cannot be truly effective unless well used by trained catechists. Thus the adequate *formation of catechists* cannot be overlooked by concerns such as the updating of texts and the re-organization of catechesis.[4]

Consequently, diocesan pastoral programmes must give absolute priority to the *formation of lay catechists.* Together with this, a fundamentally decisive element must be the *catechetical formation of priests* both at the level of seminary formation as well as at the level of continuing formation. Bishops are called upon to ensure that they are scrupulously attentive to such formation.

---

[3] Cf. GMC, 5.
[4] DCG (1971) 108a.

Nature and purpose of the formation of catechists

235. Formation seeks to enable catechists to transmit the Gospel to those who desire to entrust themselves to Jesus Christ. The purpose of formation, therefore, is to make the catechist capable of communicating: "The summit and centre of catechetical formation lies in an aptitude and ability to communicate the Gospel message".[5]

The christocentric purpose of catechesis, which emphasizes the communion of the convert with Jesus Christ, permeates all aspects of the formation of catechists.[6] This aim is nothing other than to lead the catechist to know how to animate a catechetical journey of which, the necessary stages are: the proclamation of Jesus Christ; making known his life by setting it in the context of salvation history; explanation of the mystery of the Son of God, made man for us; and finally to help the catechumen, or those being catechized, to identify with Jesus Christ through the sacraments of initiation.[7] With continuing catechesis, the catechist merely tries to deepen these basic elements. This christological perspective touches directly upon the identity of the catechist and his preparation. *"The unity and harmony of the catechist must be read in this christocentric light and built around a profound familiarity with Christ and the Father, in the Spirit".*[8]

236. By virtue of the fact that formation seeks to make the catechist capable of transmitting the Gospel in the name of the

[5] Cf. DCG (1971) 111.
[6] Cf. CT 5c. This text defines the christocentric end of catechesis. This fact determines the Christocentric content of catechesis. It also determines the christocentricity of the response of those to whom catechesis is addressed (the 'Yes' to Jesus Christ) and the christocentricity of the spirituality of the catechist and of his formation.
[7] The four stages of the baptismal catechumenate are cultivated in a christocentric prospective.
[8] *Guide for Catechists,* 20.

Church, all formation has an ecclesial nature. The formation of catechists is nothing other than an assistance for them in identifying with the living and actual awareness that the Church has of the Gospel, in order to make them capable of transmitting it in his name.

In concrete terms, the catechist—in his formation—enters into communion with that aspiration of the Church which, like a spouse, "keeps pure and intact the faith of the Spouse"[9] and which, as "mother and teacher" desires to transmit the Gospel by adapting it to all cultures, ages, and situations. This truly ecclesial quality of the transmission of the Gospel permeates the entire formation of catechists and gives to that formation its true nature.

The inspiring criteria of the formation of catechists

237. An adequate conception of the formation of catechists must always take prior note of some of the criteria which inspire and configure with varying emphases relevant to the formation of catechists:

– Firstly, it is a question of forming catechists for the need to evangelize in the present historical context, with its values, challenges and disappointments. To accomplish this task, it is necessary for catechists to have a deep faith,[10] a clear Christian and ecclesial identity;[11] as well as a great social sensitivity.[12] All formation programmes must accommodate these points.

– In formation, account must also be taken of the *concept of catechesis*, proposed by the Church today. It is a question of

[9] LG 64.
[10] DCG (1971) 114.
[11] Cf. *Guide for Catechists*, 7.
[12] Cf. *Guide for Catechists*, 13.

forming catechists so as to be able to transmit not only a teaching but also an integral Christian formation, by developing "tasks of initiation, of education, and of teaching".[13] Catechists must be able to be, at one and the same time, teachers, educators and witnesses of the faith.

– The present *catechetical moment* being lived by the Church requires catechists who can "integrate", who are capable of overcoming "unilateral divergent tendencies"[14] and who are able to provide a full and complete catechesis. They must know how to link the dimension of truth and meaning of the faith, orthodoxy and orthopraxis, ecclesial and social meaning. Formation must contribute to the enrichment of these factors lest tensions arise between them.

– The formation of lay catechists cannot ignore the *specific character of the laity in the Church,* and cannot be regarded as merely a synthesis of the mission received by priests and religious. Rather, "their apostolic training acquires a special character precisely from the secular nature of the lay state and from its particular type of spirituality".

– Finally, the *pedagogy* used in this formation is of fundamental importance. As a general criterion, it is necessary to underline the need for a coherence between the general pedagogy of formation of catechists and the pedagogy proper to the catechetical process. It would be very difficult for the catechist in his activity to improvise a style and a sensibility to which he had not been introduced during his own formation.

---

[13] DCG (1971) 31.
[14] CT 52; cf. CT 22.

The dimensions of formation: being, knowing, and savoir-faire

238.   The formation of catechists is made up of different dimensions. The deepest dimension refers to the very being of the
catechist, to his human and Christian dimension. Formation,
above all else, must help him to mature as a person, a believer
and as an apostle. This is what the catechist must know so as to
be able to fulfil his responsibilities well. This dimension is permeated by the double commitment he has to the message and to
man. It requires the catechist to have a sufficient knowledge of
the message that he transmits and of those to whom he transmits
the message and of the social context in which they live. This
then is the dimension of *savoir-faire,* of knowing how to transmit
the message, so that it is an act of communication. The formation of the catechist tends to make of him an "educator of man
and of the life of man".[15]

The human, Christian and apostolic maturity of catechists.

239.   On the basis of this initial human maturity,[16] the exercise
of catechesis, by constant consideration and evaluation, allows the
catechist to grow in a balanced and in a critical outlook, in integrity, in his ability to relate, to promote dialogue, to have a
constructive spirit, and to engage in group work.[17] It will cause
him to grow in respect and in love for catechumens and those
being catechized: "What is this love? It is the love, not so much
of a teacher as of a father, or rather of a mother. It is the
Lord's wish that every preacher of the Gospel, every builder up

---

[15] CT 22d.
[16] Cf. GCM, 21.
[17] The following human qualities are suggested by the *Guide for Catechists*: facility in
human relationships and dialogue facilitating communication, a disposition to collaboration, a willingness to act as a guide, serenity of judgement, understanding and
realism, a capacity to give consolation and hope (cf. 21).

of the Church should have this love".[18] Formation also assumes that the faith of the catechist is fostered and nourished by the exercize of catechesis, making him thus to grow as a believer. The formation, above all, nourishes the *spirituality* of the catechist,[19] so that his activity springs in truth from his own witness of life. Every theme covered by formation should feed, in the first place, the faith of the catechist. It is true that catechists catechize others by firstly catechizing themselves.

Formation also constantly nourishes the *apostolic consciousness of the catechist,* that is, his sense of being an evangelizer. For this reason he should be aware of and live out the concrete evangelization efforts being made in his own diocese, as well as those of his own parish so as to be in harmony with the awareness that the particular Church has of its own mission. The best way to feed this apostolic awareness is by identifying with the figure of Jesus Christ, teacher and formator of disciples by seeking to acquire the zeal which Jesus had for the Kingdom. Beginning with the exercise of catechesis, the apostolic vocation of the catechist—constantly fostered by continuing formation—will progressively mature.

The biblico-theological formation of the catechist

240. Besides being a witness, the catechist must also be a teacher who teaches the faith. A biblico-theological formation should afford the catechist an organic awareness of the Christian message, structured around the central mystery of the faith, Jesus Christ.

The context of this doctrinal formation should be drawn from the various areas that constitute every catechetical programme;

---

[18] EN 79.
[19] Cf. ChL 60.

– the three great eras in the history of Salvation: the Old Testament, the life of Christ and the history of the Church.

– the great nuclei of the Christian message: the Creed, the Liturgy, the moral life and prayer.

In its own level of theological instruction, the doctrinal content of the formation of a catechist is that which the catechist must transmit. For its part, "Sacred Scripture should be the very soul of this formation".[20] The *Catechism of the Catholic Church* remains the fundamental doctrinal reference point together with the catechism proper to the particular Church.

241.   This biblico-theological formation must contain certain qualities:

a) In the first place, it should be of a summary nature and correspond to the message to be transmitted. The various elements of the Christian faith should be presented in a well structured way and in harmony with each other by means of an organic vision that respects the "hierarchy of truths".

b) This synthesis of faith should be such as to help the catechist to mature in his own faith and enable him to offer an explanation for the present hope in this time of mission: "The situation today points to an ever-increasing urgency for doctrinal formation of the lay faithful, not simply for a better understanding which is natural to faith's dynamism, but also in enabling them to 'give a reason for their hope' in view of the world and its grave and complex problems".[21]

---

[20] Cf. DCG (1971) 112. *Guide for Catechists,* 23, underlines the primary importance of Sacred Scripture in the formation of catechists: "May Sacred Scripture continue to be the principal subject of teaching and may it become the soul of all theological study. Where necessary may this be actualized".

[21] ChL 60c.

c) It must be a theological formation that is close to human experience and capable of correlating the various aspects of the Christian message with the concrete life of man "both to inspire it and to judge it in the light of the Gospel".[22] While remaining theological it must in some fashion adopt a catechetical style.

d) It must be such that the catechist "will be able not only to communicate the Gospel accurately, but also able to make those being taught capable of receiving it actively and of discerning what in their spiritual journey agrees with the faith".[23]

The human sciences and the formation of catechists

242. The catechist also acquires a knowledge of man and the reality in which he lives through the human sciences which have greatly developed in our own time. "In pastoral care sufficient use should be made, not only of theological principles, but also of secular findings, especially in the fields of psychology and sociology: in this way the faithful will be brought to a more mature living of the faith".[24]

It is necessary for the catechist to have some contact, with at least some of the fundamental elements of psychology: the psychological dynamics motivating man; personality structure; the deepest needs and aspirations of the human heart; progressive psychology and the phases of the human life-cycle; the psychology of religion and the experiences which open man to the mystery of the sacred.

The social sciences provide an awareness of the socio-cultural context in which man lives and by which he is strongly influenced. It is therefore necessary that in the formation of catechists

---

[22] CT 22.
[23] DCG (1971) 112.
[24] GS 62b.

that there take place "an analysis of the religious situation as well as of the sociological, cultural and economic conditions to the extent that these facts of collective life can greatly influence the success of evangelization".[25] In addition to these sciences, explicitly recommended by the Second Vatican Council, other human sciences should be used in one way or another in the formation of catechists, particularly the sciences of education and communication.

Various criteria which can inspire the use of human sciences in the formation of catechists

243. These are:

a) Respect for the autonomy of the sciences: "the Church... affirms the legitimate autonomy of culture and especially of the sciences".[26]

b) Evangelical discernment of the different tendencies or schools in psychology, sociology, and pedagogy: their values and their limitations.

c) The study of the human sciences—in the formation of catechists—is not an end in itself. Acquiring awareness of the existential, psychological, cultural and social situation of man is accomplished in the light of the faith in which man must be educated.[27]

---

[25] DCG (1971) 100.

[26] GS 59.

[27] "In the teaching of human sciences, given their very great number and diversity there are difficult problems in regard to choosing from among them and in regard to the method of teaching them. Since the question here is one of training catechists, not experts in psychology, the norm to be followed is this: determine and choose that which can directly help them to acquire facility in communication." DCG (1971) 112.

d) In forming catechists, theology and the human sciences should mutually enrich each other. Consequetly it is necessary to avoid a situation in which these materials are converted into the only norm for the pedagogy of the faith apart from the theological criteria deriving from the divine pedagogy. While these are fundamental and necessary disciplines, they are always at theservice of evangelization which is more than a human activity.[28]

Pedagogical formation

244. Together with those dimensions which refer to being and knowledge, the formation of catechists must also cultivate *technique*. The catechist is an educator who facilitates maturation of the faith which catechumens and those being catechized obtain with the help of the Holy Spirit.[29] The first reality of which account must be taken in this decisive area of formation is that concerning the original pedagogy of faith. The catechist is prepared or formed so as to facilitate a growth in the experience of faith, which he himself has not implanted for it is God who has sown it in the heart of man. The responsibility of the catechist is

---

[28] A fundamental text for use of the human sciences in the formation of catechists continues to be that recommended by the Second Vatican Council in GS 62: "The faithful ought to work in close conjunction with their contemporaries and try to get to know that their ways of thinking and feeling, as they find them expressed in current culture. Let the faithful incorporate the findings of new sciences and teachings and the understanding of the most recent discoveries with Christian morality and thought so that their practice of religion and their moral behaviour may keep abreast of their acquaintance with science and of the relentless progress of technology: in this way they will succeed in evaluating and interpreting everything with an authentically Christian sense of values".

[29] The importance of pedagogy is underlined by CT 58: "Among the many prestigious sciences of man that are nowadays making immense advances, pedagogy is certainly one of the most important... the science of education and the art of teaching are continually being subjected to review, with a view to making them better adapted or more effective, with varying degrees of success".

merely to cultivate this gift by nourishing it and by helping it to grow.[30] Formation seeks to mature an educational capacity in the catechist which implies: an ability to be attentive to people, an ability to interpret or respond to educational tasks or initiatives in organizing learning activities and the ability of leading a human group toward maturity. As with any other art the most important factor is that the catechist should acquire his own style of imparting catechesis by adapting the general principles of catechetical pedagogy to his own personality.[31]

245. More concretely: it must enable the catechist and particularly the full-time catechist to know how to organize in the group of catechists, educational activity by carefully considering the circumstances, by elaborating a realistic catechetical plan and—having drawn it up—to know how to evaluate it critically.[32] It must be capable of animating a group by applying with discernment the techniques of group dynamics offered by psychology. This educational capacity and this "know-how" along with the knowledge, attitudes and techniques which it involves "can be better acquired if they are taught simultaneously while the apostolic works are being performed (for example, during sessions when lessons of catechesis are being prepared and tested)".[33] The goal or ideal is that catechists should be the protagonists of their own learning by being creative in formation and not by just applying external rules. This formation must be closely related to praxis: one must start with praxis to be able to arrive at praxis.[34]

[30] Cf. CT 58.
[31] Cf. DCG (1971) 113.
[32] *Ibid.*
[33] DCG (1971) 112.
[34] Cf. GCM, 28.

The formation of catechists within the Christian community

246. Among the ways of forming catechists, those of their own Christian community are all important. It is in this community that catechists test their own vocation and continually nourish their own apostolic awareness. The figure of the priest is fundamental in the task of assuring their progressive maturation as believers and witnesses.[35]

247. A Christian community can develop various types of formative activities for their own catechists:

a) One of these is the constant fostering of the ecclesial vocation of catechists by keeping alive in them an awareness of being sent by the Church;

b) It is also important to ensure catechists have a mature faith, through the usual means by which the Christian community educates in the faith its own pastoral workers and its more committed lay members.[36] When the faith of catechists is not yet mature it is advisable that they should participate in a catechumenal programme designed for young people and adults. This can be organized by the community itself, or one specifically created for them.

c) Immediate preparation for catechesis, done with a group of catechists, is an excellent means of formation especially when accompanied with an evaluation of all that has been experienced in the sessions of catechesis.

d) Within the community other formative activities can also be realized: courses in awareness of catechesis, for example, at

---

[35] "Priests and religious ought to assist the lay faithful in their formation. In this regard the Synod Fathers have invited priests and candidates for Orders 'to be prepared carefully so they are ready to foster the vocation and mission of the lay faithful'". ChL 61.

[36] Cf. ChL 61.

the beginning of the pastoral year; retreats and living in community at the important liturgical times of the year; [37] dissertations on more pressing and necessary themes; systematic doctrinal formation, for example, studying the *Catechism of the Catholic Church.* These are activities of continuing formation, which together with the personal work of the catechist, would appear very useful.[38]

Schools for catechists and centres for higher learning for experts in catechesis

248.   Attendance at a *school for catechists* [39] is a particularly important moment in the formation of a catechist. In many places such schools are organized on two levels: one for catechists who are "ordinary"; [40] the other for those who have "responsibility for catechesis".

Schools for ordinary catechists

249.   The purpose of such schools is to give an comprehensive and systematic catechetical formation of a basic nature over a period of time during which the specifically catechetical dimensions of formation are promoted: the Christian message; knowledge of man and his socio-cultural situation; the pedagogy of the faith. Such a systematic formation has notable advantages amongst which the following can be numbered:

[37] "Also to be recommended are those parochial initiatives that promote the interior formation of catechists, such as prayer groups, the fraternal life, spiritual sharing and spiritual retreats. These initiatives do not isolate catechists but they help them to grow in their own spirituality and in communion with one another" (GCM, 22).

[38] Cf. DCG (1971) 110.

[39] Cf. concerning schools for catechists in the missions: AG 17c; RM 73; CIC 785 and GCM, 30. For the Church in general see: DCG (1971) 109.

[40] The expression 'ordinary catechist' is used in DCG (1971) 112c.

– its systematic nature which is not so absorbed in the immediate concerns of catechetical activity;

– its quality which is assured by trained specialists;

– integration with catechists from other communities, which promotes ecclesial communion.

Institutes for those with responsibility for catechesis

250. So as to prepare those who have responsibility for catechesis, in parishes and vicariates as well as full time catechists [41] it is useful to provide catechetical institutes either at diocesan or inter-diocesan level. Clearly, standards in these institutes will be more demanding. In addition to the courses of basic catechetical formation they will promote those specializations regarded as necessary for the particular circumstances in which they are located. It may prove opportune, even for reasons of rationalizing resources, that the orientation of such institutes be directed towards those with responsibility for various pastoral activities. In this event they can be transformed into *centres of formation for pastoral workers.* Commencing with a general basic formation (doctrinal and anthropological) those areas in which specialization is required should be determined in relation to the particular demands made on the various pastoral and apostolic works of the diocese in which its pastoral workers are involved.

Higher institutes for experts in catechesis

251. A higher level of catechetical formation to which priests, religious and laity might have access is of vital importance for catechesis. In this regard it is hoped that "higher institutes for training in pastoral catechetics should be promoted or founded,

[41] Cf. DCG (1971) 109b.

so that catechists capable of directing catechesis at the diocesan level, or within the area of activities to which religious congregations are dedicated, may be prepared. These higher institutes can be national or even international. They ought to function as a university so far as curriculum, length of course and requisites for admission are concerned".[42] In addition to the formation of those who must assume responsibility for catechesis, these institutes will also form those who teach catechesis in seminaries, houses of formation and in the catechetical schools. These institutes should devote themselves to a congruent level of research in catechesis.

252. At this level of formation there is much opportunity for fruitful co-operation between the Churches: "Here also the material aid provided by the richer Churches to their poorer sisters can show the greatest effectiveness, for what better assistance can one Church give to another than to help it to grow as a Church with its own strength?"[43] Obviously such collaboration has due respect for the particular circumstances of poorer Churches and their responsibilities. At diocesan and inter-diocesan levels it is most useful when there is an awareness of the need to form people at a higher level, just as there is a similar need for such in other ecclesiastical activities as well as in the teaching of other disciplines.

---

[42] DCG (1971) 109a.
[43] CT 71a.

CHAPTER III

Loci and means of catechesis

The Christian community is a home for catechesis [1]

253. The Christian community is the historical realization of the gift of "communion" (*koinonia*), [2] which is a fruit of the Holy Spirit. "Communion" expresses the profound nucleus between the universal Church and the particular Churches which make up the Christian community. It is realized and made visible in the rich variety of immediate Christian communities in which Christians are born into the faith, educated in it and live it: the family; parish; Catholic schools; Christian associations and movements; basic ecclesial communities. These are the loci of catechesis, the community places where initiatory catechesis and continuing education in the faith are realized. [3]

254. The Christian community is the origin, locus and goal of catechesis. Proclamation of the Gospel always begins with the Christian community and invites man to conversion and the following of Christ. It is the same community that welcomes those who wish to know the Lord better and permeate themselves with a new life. The Christian community accompanies catechumens and those being catechized, and with maternal solicitude

---

[1] See Part Five, chap. 1 where mention is made of the community responsibility for catechesis. This is regarded as a locus of catechizing.
[2] Cf. CONGREGATION FOR THE DOCTRINE OF THE FAITH, *"Communionis notio"*, n. 1: *l.c.* 838.
[3] Cf. MPD 13.

makes them participate in her own experience of the faith and incorporates them into herself.[4]

Catechesis is always the same. However the *loci* [5] of catechesis distinguish it, each in its own way. Hence it is important to know the role of each of these.

The family as an environment or means of growth in faith

255. Parents are the primary educators in the faith. Together with them, especially in certain cultures, all members of the family play an active part in the education of the younger members. It is thus necessary to determine more concretely the sense in which the Christian family community is a *locus* of catechesis. The family is defined as a "domestic Church",[6] that is, in every Christian family the different aspects and functions of the life of the entire Church may be reflected: mission; catechesis; witness; prayer etc. Indeed in the same way as the Church, the family "is a place in which the Gospel is transmitted and from which it extends".[7] The family as a *locus* of catechesis has an unique privilege: transmitting the Gospel by rooting it in the context of profound human values.[8] On this human base, Christian initiation is more profound: the awakening of the sense of God; the first steps in prayer; education of the moral conscience; formation in the Christian sense of human love, understood as a reflection of the love of God the Father, the Creator. It is, indeed, a Christian education more witnessed to than taught, more occasional than systematic, more on-going and daily than structured

---

[4] Cf. CT 24.
[5] CT 67a. This is a classic expression in catechesis. The Apostolic Exhortation speaks of the places of catechesis (*de locis catecheseos*).
[6] Cf LG 11; cf AA 11; FC 49.
[7] EN 71.
[8] Cf. GS 52; FC 37a.

into periods. In this family catechesis, the role of grandparetns is of growing importace. Their wisdom and sense of the religious is often times decisive in creating a true Christian climate.

The baptismal catechumenate of adults [9]

256. The baptismal catechumenate is a typical *locus* of catechesis, instituted by the Church to prepare adults, who desire to become Christians and to receive the Sacraments of Christian initiation.[10] In the catechumenate, it is realized "that specific formation by means of which the adult, converted to the faith, is brought to a confession of baptismal faith during the Easter Vigil".[11] The catechesis given in the catechumenate is closely linked with the Christian community.[12] From the moment of their entry into the catechumenate, the Church surrounds catechumens "with her affection, her care, as though they are already her children and joined to her: indeed, they belong to the family of Christ".[13] Thus the Christian community assists "candidates and catechumens during their initiation process, from the precatechumenate to the catechumenate, to the period of mystagogy".[14] This continual presence of the Christian community is expressed in different ways and appropriately described in the *Rite of Christian Initiation of Adults.*[15]

---

[9] See Part I, chap. III. Here the question of the baptismal catechumenate as a locus of catechesis is addressed in relation to the continuing presence of the community in it.

[10] Cf. DCG (1971), 130 which describes the end of the baptismal catechumenate. Cf. RCIA 4 indicates the connection between the baptismal catechumenate and the Christian community.

[11] Synod, MPG 8c.

[12] Cf. RCIA 4, 41.

[13] RCIA 18.

[14] RCIA 41.

[15] Cf. RCIA 41.

The parish as an environment for catechesis

257. The parish is, without doubt, the most important *locus* in which the Christian community is formed and expressed. This is called to be a fraternal and welcoming family where Christians become aware of being the people of God.[16] In the parish, all human differences melt away and are absorbed into the universality of the Church.[17] The parish is also the usual place in which the faith is born and in which it grows. It constitutes, therefore, a very adequate community space for the realization of the ministry of the word at once as teaching, education and life experience.

Today, the parish is undergoing profound transformation in many countries. Social changes are having repercussions on the parish especially in big cities "shaken by the phenomenon of urbanization".[18] Despite this, "the parish is still a major point of reference for the Christian people, even for the non-practising".[19] It must however, continue " to be the prime mover and pre-eminent place for catechesis",[20] while recognising that in certain occasions, it cannot be the centre of gravity for all of the ecclesial functions of catechesis and must integrate itself into other institutions.

258. In order that the parish may succeed in activating effectively the mission of evangelization, some conditions must be fulfilled:

a) Adult catechesis[21] must be given priority. This involves "a post-baptismal catechesis, in the form of a catechumenate, ...pre-

---

[16] Cf. CT 67c.
[17] Cf. AA 10.
[18] CT 67b.
[19] *Ibid.*
[20] *Ibid.*
[21] The importance of adult catechesis is underlined in CT 43 and DCG (1971) 20.

senting again some elements from the *Rite of Christian Initiation of Adults* with the purpose of allowing a person to grasp and live the immense, extraordinary richness and responsibility received at Baptism".[22]

b) With renewed courage, the proclamation of the Gospel to those alienated or who live in religious indifference[23] must be planned. In this task, pre-sacramental meetings (*preparation for Marriage, Baptism and First Holy Communion of children*) can be fundamental.[24]

c) As a solid reference point for parochial catechesis it is necessary to have a nucleus of mature Christians, initiated into the faith, to whom different pastoral concerns can be entrusted. This objective can be more easily achieved by the formation of small ecclesial communities.[25]

d) While the preceding points refer mainly to adults, at the same time catechesis for children, adolescents, and young people—which is always indispensable—will also benefit greatly.

Catholic schools

259. The Catholic school[26] is a most important *locus* for human and Christian formation. The declaration of the Second Vatican

---

[22] ChL 61.
[23] Cf. EN 52.
[24] Cf. DCG (1971) 96c.
[25] It is important to state as Pope John Paul II does in ChL 61 the usefulness of small ecclesial groups in the context of parishes. They should not however be a parallel movement which absorbs the best members of parishes: "internal to the parish, especially if vast and territorially extensive, small Church communities, where present, can be a notable help in the formation of Christians by providing a consciousness and an experience of ecclesial communion and mission which are more extensive and incisive".
[26] Cf. CONGREGATION FOR CATHOLIC EDUCATION, *The Catholic School*, Rome 1977.

Council, *Gravissimum Educationis* "makes a decisive change in the
history of Catholic schools: the move from school as institution
to school as community".[27] Catholic schools "are no less zealous
than other schools in the promotion of culture and in the human
formation of young people. It is however, the special function of
the Catholic school to:

– develop in the school community an atmosphere animated
by a spirit of liberty and charity;

– enable young people, while developing their own personality, to grow at the same time in that new life which has been
given them in baptism;

– orientate the whole of human culture to the message of salvation"; [28]

The educational task of Catholic schools is bound to be developed along the basis of this concept proposed by the Second
Vatican Council. It is accomplished in the school community, to
which belong all of those who are directly involved in it: "teachers, management, administrative and auxiliary staff, parents—central in that they are the natural and irreplaceable educators of
their own children—and pupils, who are participants and active
subjects too of the educational process".[29]

260.   When most students attending a Catholic school belong to
families who associate themselves with the school because of its
Catholic character, the ministry of the word can be exercised in
it in multiple forms: primary proclamation, scholastic religious instruction, catechesis, homily. Two of these forms, however, have

---

[27] CONGREGATION FOR CATHOLIC EDUCATION, *The religious dimension of education
in the Catholic School. Outlines for Reflection,* Rome 1988, n. 31.
[28] GE 28.
[29] CONGREGATION FOR CATHOLIC EDUCATION, *The Religions dimension of education in the Catholic School, n. 32: l.c.*

a particular importance in the Catholic school: religious instruction in the school and catechesis whose respective characteristics have already been discussed.[30] When students and their families become associated with Catholic schools because of the quality of education offered in the school, or for other possible reasons, catechetical activity is necessarily limited and even religious education—when possible—accentuates its cultural character. The contribution of such schools is always "a service of great value to men",[31] as well as an internal element of evangelization of the Church. Given the plurality of socio-cultural and religious contexts in which the work of Catholic schools is carried on in different nations, it is opportune that the Bishops and the Episcopal Conferences specify the kind of catechetical activity to be implemented in Catholic schools.

Associations, movements and groups of the faithful

261. The purpose of the various "associations, movements and groups of the faithful" [32] which develop in a particular Church is to help the disciples of Jesus Christ to fulfil their lay mission in the world and in the Church. In such associations Christians devote themselves to "the practice of piety, the direct apostolate, charity and relief work, or a Christian presence in temporal matters".[33] In all of these associations and movements it is always necessary to provide formation of some kind, in order to culti-

[30] *"The special character of the Catholic school, the underlying reason for it, the reason why Catholic parents should prefer it, is precisely the quality of the religious instruction integrated into the education of the pupils"* (CT 69); cf Part I, Chap. 2, nn. 73-76.
[31] AG 12c.
[32] Cf. CT 70.
[33] CT 70 mentions those associations, movements and groups of faithful in which the catechetical aspects of their formation are attended to but which do not give rise, properly speaking, to environments of chatechizing.

vate the fundamental aspects of the Christian life: "In fact they
have the possibility, each with its own method, of offering a formation through a deeply shared experience in the apostolic life
as well as having the opportunity to integrate, to make concrete
and specific the formation that their members receive from other
persons and communities".[34] Catechesis is always a basic dimension in the formation of the laity. Usually, these organizations
have "special times for catechesis".[35] Such catechesis is not an al-
ternative for Christian formation. Rather it is one of its fundamental aspects.

262. When catechesis is given in the context of these associations and movements, some important aspects of it must be regarded as fundamental:

a) The "proper nature" [36] of catechesis must be respected by
developing the richness of its content through the threefold dimension of word, memory and witness (doctrine, celebration and
commitment in life).[37] Catechesis, whatever the "way" in which it
is given, is always a basic organic formation in the faith. It must,
however, include "a serious study of Christian doctrine",[38] and it
must constitute a serious religious formation "open to all the...
factors of the Christian life".[39]

b) This is not an impediment to accomplishing the objectives
proper to the various associations and movements—with their

[34] ChL 62.
[35] CT 67.
[36] CT 47b.
[37] CT 47b.
[38] CT 47. In this text Pope John Paul II speaks of diverse groups of young people:
groups of Catholic action, prayer groups, groups for Christian reflection... he asks
that in these there should also be a serious study of Christian doctrine. Catechesis
should always be considered an essential part in the apostolic life of the laity.
[39] Cf. CT 21.

own charisms. With different emphases, catechesis must always remain faithful to its own nature. Education in the spirituality proper to a particular movement or association enriches the Church and is a natural continuation of the basic formation received by all Christians. Firstly, it is necessary to educate in what is common to all the members of the Church, before educating in what is particular and diverse.

c) It is necessary to affirm that movements and associations, as far as catechesis is concerned, are not alternatives to the parish since this is the educational community to which reference must be made by catechesis.[40]

Basic ecclesial communities

263. Basic ecclesial communities have experienced a great diffusion in recent decades.[41] These are groups of Christians which "arise because men want to live the life of the Church with greater fervour or because they desire and seek a more human way of life which large ecclesial communities cannot easily provide".[42]

Basic ecclesial communities are a sign of the "Church's vitality".[43] The disciples of Christ gather together in them so as to hear the word of God, to develop fraternal bonds, to celebrate the Christian mysteries in their lives and to assume responsibility for transforming society. In addition to these specifically Christian concerns other important human values emerge: friendship, personal recognition, a spirit of co-responsibility, creativity, vocational response, concern for the problems of the world and of

---

[40] Cf. CT 67b-c.
[41] EN 58 indicates how basic ecclesial communities flourish nearly everywhere in the Church. RM 51 refers to them as a phenomenon in rapid growth.
[42] EN 58c.
[43] RM 51a; cf. EN 58f; LC 69.

the Church. From them, an enriched community experience can result, "a true expression of communion and a means for the construction of a more profound communion".[44] To be authentic, "every community must live in union with the particular and the universal Church, in heartfelt communion with the Church's Pastors and the Magisterium, with a commitment to missionary outreach and without yielding to isolationism or ideological exploitation".[45]

264. In basic ecclesial communities an extremely enriching catechesis can be developed:

– The fraternal climate, in which it lives, is an environment suitable for integral catechetical activity, providing that the proper nature and character of catechesis is respected;

– On the other hand, catechesis must strive to deepen community life so as to ensure a basis for the Christian life of the faithful, without which basic Christian communities lack stability;

– The small Community is always a suitable place to receive those who have concluded a catechetical journey.

[44] RM 51c.
[45] *Ibid.*, RM 51; cf. EN 58; LC 69.

CHAPTER IV

The organization of catechetical pastoral care in the particular Churches

ORGANIZATION AND EXERCISE OF RESPONSIBILITIES

The diocesan service of catechesis

265. The organization of catechetical pastoral care has as its reference point the Bishop and the Diocese. The diocesan catechetical office *(Officium Catechisticum)* is "the means which the Bishop as head of the community and teacher of doctrine utilizes to direct and moderate all the catechetical activities of the diocese". [1]

266. The principal competencies of the diocesan office are the following:

a) to analyse the state of the diocese [2] with regard to education in the faith: such analysis must identify, amongst other things, the real needs of the diocese as far as catechetical praxis is concerned;

b) to develop a plan of action [3] which sets out clear objectives, proposes definite suggestions and shows concrete results;

---

[1] DCG (1971) 126. The diocesan office *(officium catechisticum)* was instituted in every diocese by the decree *Provido Sane* (1935): cf. AAS 27 (1935), p. 151; see also CIC 775 § 1.

[2] Cf. DCG (1971) 100. the general lines are suggested in the *Introduction* and also in this chapter under the heading: *Analysis of the situation and of needs*.

[3] Cf. DCG (1971) 103. See also in this chapter: *"Programmes of catechetical actions and orientation"*.

c) to promote the formation of catechist: in this respect suitable centres shall be set up; [4]

d) to elaborate, or at least to indicate to parishes and to catechists, the necessary instruments for catechesis: catechisms, directories, programmes for different ages, guides for catechists, material for those being catechized, audio-visual aids etc.; [5]

e) to foster diocesan institutions of a specifically catechetical character (*catechumenate, parochial catechesis, groups responsible for catechesis*): these are the "basic cells" [6] of catechetical activity;

f) to improve personnel and material resources at diocesan level as well as at the level of the parish and the vicariates forane; [7]

g) to collaborate with the Liturgical Office given the relevance of Liturgy for catechesis, especially for catechumenal and initiatory catechesis.

267.   To accomplish these responsibilities, the diocesan catechetical office should "have a staff of persons who have special competence. The extent and the diversity of the problems which must be handled demand that the responsibilities be divided among a number of truly skilled people". [8] Ordinarily, this diocesan service should be performed by priests, religious and laity. Catechesis is so basic to the life of every particular Church, that "no diocese can be without its own catechetical office". [9]

---

[4] Cf. DCG (1971) 108-109. See also Part V, chapter II.
[5] Cf. DCG (1971) 116-124.
[6] DCG (1971) 126.
[7] Cf. CT 63. Pope John Paul II recommends that catechesis be given *"pertinent and effective organization, putting in to operation the necessary personnel, means and equipment, and also financial resources"*.
[8] DCG (1971) 126.
[9] *Ibidem.*

Services of inter-diocesan co-operation

268. This co-operation is extremely fruitful in our time. Shared catechetical endeavour is advisable not only for reasons of geographic proximity but also for reasons of cultural homogeneity. Indeed "it is useful for a number of Dioceses to combine their actions, bringing together for common benefit their experiences and undertakings, their offices and equipment; for the Dioceses that are better provided to give help to the others; and for a common action programme to be prepared for the region as a whole".[10]

The service of the Episcopal Conference

269. "The Episcopal Conference may establish a catechetical office, whose principal purpose is to assist individual dioceses in catechetical matters".[11] This possibility, which has been established by the *Code of Canon Law,* is in fact a reality in many of the Episcopal Conferences. The catechetical office or national catechetical centre of the Episcopal Conference has a double function: [12]

– to be at the service of the catechetical needs of all Dioceses of a given territory: it oversees publications of national relevance, national congresses, relations with the mass media and, in general, those tasks and responsibilities which are beyond the means of Dioceses or regions;

– to be at the service of the Dioceses and regions by distributing information and catechetical projects, in order to co-ordinate activities and to lend assistance to Dioceses less well provided with catechetical materials.

[10] DCG (1971) 127.
[11] CIC 775 § 3.
[12] Cf. DCG (1971) 129.

If an Episcopate so determines, it is also within the competence of the catechetical office or the national catechetical centre to co-ordinate its activities with other catechetical institutions or to co-operate with catechetical activities at international level. All this, however, is always done as a means of assistance to the Bishops of an Episcopal Conference.

The service of the Holy See

270. "The command of Christ to preach the Gospel to every creature applies primarily and immediately to them (the Bishops)—with Peter, and subject to Peter".[13] The ministry of the Successor of Peter—in this collegial mandate of Jesus regarding the proclamation and transmission of the Gospel—assumes a basic responsibility. This ministry must be considered "not only as a global service reaching every Church *from the outside,* but *from inside* as something already belonging to the essence of every particular Church".[14]

The ministry of Peter in catechesis is exercised in an eminent way through its teachings. The Pope, in what regards catechesis, acts in an immediate and particular way through the Congregation for Clergy, which assists "the Roman Pontiff in the exercise of his supreme pastoral office".[15]

---

[13] AG 38a; cf. CIC 756 §§ 1-2.

[14] JOHN PAUL II, *Allocution* to the Bishops of the United States of America, during the meeting in the seminary of Our Lady of Los Ageles 16-IX-1987: *Insegnamenti di Giovanni Paolo II,* X, 3 (1987), 556. The expression is taken from the CONGREGATION FOR THE DOCTRINE OF THE FAITH, *Communionis Notio,* Rome 1992, n. 13, *l.c.* 846.

[15] Apostolic Constitution *Pastor Bonus,* art. 1. This constitution, of 28 June 1988, deals with the reform of the Roman Curia which had been requested by the Council: cf. CD 9. The first reform was promulgated by the Apostolic Constitution *Regimmini Ecclesiae* of Paul VI, 18 August 1967: AAS 59 (1967) pp. 885-928.

271. The Congregation for the Clergy thus:

– "has the function of promoting the religious education of the Christian faithful of all ages and conditions;

– issues timely norms so that catechetical lessons be conducted according to a proper programme;

– maintains a watchful attention to the suitable delivery of catechetical instruction;

– grants, with the assent of the Congregation of the Doctrine of the Faith, the prescribed approbation of the Holy See for catechisms and other writings pertaining to catechetical instruction; [16]

– is available to catechetical offices and international initiatives on religious education, coordinates their activities and, where necessary, it lends assistance". [17]

THE CO-ORDINATION OF CATECHESIS

The importance of an effective co-ordination of catechesis

272. The *co-ordination of catechesis* is an important internal responsibility of the local Church. It can be considered:

– from within catechesis itself, through its diverse forms, intended for different ages and social contexts;

– in reference to the link between catechesis and other forms of education in the faith and other evangelizing activities.

The co-ordination of catechesis is not merely a strategic factor, aimed at more effective evangelization, but has a profound theological meaning. Evangelizing activity must be well co-ordinated because it touches on the *unity of faith,* which sustains all the Church's actions.

---

[16] See nn. 282 and 284 of this chapter.
[17] PB, 94.

273. The purpose of this section is to consider:

– the internal co-ordination of catechesis, so that the particular Church can offer a coherent and unified catechetical service;

– the link between missionary activity and catechumenal activity—which are mutually dependent—in the context of the mission *ad gentes* [18] or of *"new evangelization"*; [19]

– the need for well co-ordinated pastoral care in the area of education, taking account of the multiplicity of educators who address themselves to the same recipients, especially children and adolescents.

The Second Vatican Council recommended the co-ordination of all pastoral activity, so that the unity of the particular Church may shine forth all the more. [20]

Coherent diocesan catechetical programmes

274. The diocesan catechetical programme is the global catechetical project of a particular Church, which integrates, in a structured and coherent way, the diverse catechetical programmes addressed by the Diocese to different age groups. [21] In this sense, every particular Church, especially in relation to Christian initiation, should offer at least two services:

a) a single, coherent, process of Christian initiation for *children, adolescents and young people*, intimately connected with the

[18] RM 33.

[19] *Ibid.*

[20] CD 17a: "...the various forms of the apostolate should be encouraged. Close collaboration and the co-ordination of all the apostolic works under the direction of the Bishop should be promoted in the diocese as a whole or in parts of it. Thus all the undertakings and organizations, whether their object be catechetical, missionary, charitable, social, family, educational, or any other pastoral end, will act together in harmony, and the unity of the diocese will be more closely demonstrated".

[21] Cf. Part IV, chap. 2: *"Catechesis according to age"*.

sacraments of initiation already received or about to be received and linked with educational pastoral care;

b) a catechetical programme for *adults,* addressed to those Christians who need to deepen their faith in order to complete the Christian initiation begun at Baptism.

In many countries, there is also a growing need for programmes of catechesis for the *old,* for those Christians who, in the last stage of their earthly lives, desire, perhaps for the first time, to lay a solid foundation for their faith.

275. These different programmes of catechesis, each with it own socio-cultural variations, should not be organized separately as though they were "separate compartments without any communication between them".[22] It is necessary that the catechesis offered by a particular Church be well co-ordinated. Among the diverse forms of catechesis "their perfect complementarity must be fostered".[23] As has been already mentioned, the *organizing principle,* which gives coherence to the various catechetical programmes offered by a particular Church, is attention to adult catechesis. This is the axis around which revolves the catechesis of childhood and adolescence as well as that of old age.[24]

The fact that a Diocese offers within a single diocesan programme different programmes of catechesis does not imply that those to whom it is addressed need follow them one after the other. A young person who has arrived at adulthood with a well rounded faith does not need a catechumenal type of catechesis for adults, but other more solid nourishment, to assist him in permanently maturing in the faith. The same is true of those

[22] CT 45c.
[23] *Ibid.*
[24] Cf. DCG (1971) 20, where it is shown how the other forms of catechesis are ordered *(ordinantur)* to adult catechesis.

who arrive at old age with well rooted faith. Along with the provision of initiatory programmes, which are absolutely indispensable, the local Church must also provide diversified programmes of permanent catechesis for Christians adults.

Catechetical activity in the context of new evangelization

276. If catechesis is defined as a moment in the total process of evangelization, the problem inevitably arises of co-ordinating catechetical activity with the missionary activity which necessarily precedes it, as well as with the pastoral activity which follows it. There are in fact "elements which prepare for catechesis as well as those deriving from it".[25] In this respect, the link between missionary proclamation which seeks to stir up the faith, and initiatory catechesis, which seeks to deepen its roots, is decisive for evangelization. This link is, in a certain sense, more evident in the mission *ad gentes*.[26] Adults converted by the primary proclamation enter the catechumenate where they are catechized. In situations requiring *"new evangelization"*,[27] co-ordination becomes more complex because ordinary catechesis is, at times, offered to young people and adults who need a period of prior proclamation and awakening in their adherence to Christ.

Similar difficulties arise with regard to the catechesis of children and the formation of their parents.[28] At other times forms of ongoing catechesis are applied to adults who, in fact, reguire a true intiatory catechesis.

277. The current situation of evangelization requires that both activities, missionary proclamation and initiatory catechesis, be

---

[25] CT 18d.
[26] RM 33.
[27] *Ibidem.*
[28] Cf. CT 19 and 42.

conceived in a co-ordinated manner and be given, in the particular Church, through a single programme of evangelization which is both missionary and catechumenal. Today, catechesis must be seen above all as the consequence of an effective missionary proclamation. The directives of the decree *Ad Gentes*—which sets the catechumenate in the context of the Church's missionary activity—remain a particularly valid reference point for catechesis.[29]

Catechesis in educational pastoral work

278.   Pastoral care offered by a particular Church in the area of education should establish a necessary co-ordination between the different *loci* in which education in the faith takes place. It is extremely important that all catechetical means "should converge on the same confession of faith, on the same membership of the Church, and on commitments in society lived in the same Gospel spirit".[30] Educational co-ordination primarily concerns children, adolescents, and young adults. It is more than useful for the particular Church to integrate various educational sectors and environments in a single project at the service of the Christian education of youth. All of these *loci* complement each other, but no one of them, taken separately, can ensure a complete Christian education. Since it is always the same and unique person of the child or young person who undergoes these different educational actions, it is important that the different influences always have the same fundamental inspiration. Any contradiction between these actions is harmful, in so far as each one of them has its own specificity and importance. Thus it is most important for the particular Church to provide a programme of Christian

---

[29] Cf. AG 11-15. The concept of evangelization as a process structured in stages was analysed in Part I, chap. I. *The process of evagelization.*
[30] CT 67b.

initiation which takes into account and integrates the various educational tasks as well as the demands of new evagelization.

SOME RESPONSIBILITIES PROPER TO THE CATECHETICAL MINISTRY

Analysis of the situation and its needs

279.   The particular Church, in organizing its catechetical activity, must have as its point of departure an *analysis of the situation*. "The object of this investigation is multiple: included are examination of pastoral action and analysis of the religious situation as well as of the sociological, cultural, and economic conditions, to the extent that these facts of collective life can greatly influence the success of evangelization".[31] This is nothing other than becoming aware of reality from the point of view of catechesis and its needs.

More concretely:

– there must be a clear awareness, in *"examining pastoral action"*, of the state of catechesis: how, in fact, it is situated in the process of evangelization; a distinct balance between the various catechetical sectors (children, adolescents, young people, adults); the co-ordination of catechesis with Christian education in the family, in schools and elsewhere; its internal quality; the contents imparted and the methodology used; the characteristics of catechists and their formation;

– an *"analysis of the religious situation"* of the Diocese includes three closely related levels: the *sense of the sacred*, that is those human experiences, which, because of their depth, tend to open to mystery; the *religious sense*, the concrete ways in which a particular people conceives of and communicates with God; and

[31] DCG (1971) 100.

the *situation of the faith,* in the light of the various types of believer; in connection with these levels, it also investigates the *moral situation* as lived, inquiring into its emerging values and evident ambiguities or counter values.

– *"socio-cultural analysis"*, about which much has already been said in relation to the human sciences in the formation of catechists,[32] is also necessary because catechumens and those being catechized must be prepared to constitute a Christian presence in society.

280. The analysis of the situation, from these various perspectives, "should also convince those who work in the ministry of the word that, so far as pastoral action is concerned, human situations are ambivalent. Therefore, workers in the service of the Gospel should learn to note the many possibilities that are opening up for their action in new and diverse circumstances... For always possible is a process of change which can make clear the way to the Faith".[33]

This analysis is a primary working instrument, of an informational nature, offered by the catechetical service to pastors and catechists.

Programme of catechetical actions and orientation

281. Following close study of the situation, it becomes necessary to proceed to the formulation of a *programme of action*. This will determine the objectives, the means of pastoral catechesis and the norms governing it with reference to local needs and be in complete harmony with the objectives and norms of the universal Church. The programme or plan of action should be effective since its purpose is to orientate diocesan or inter-diocesan

---

[32] Cf. Part Five, chap. 5.
[33] DCG (1971) 102; cf. Introductory explanation, 16.

catechesis. Because of its nature, it is usually drawn up for a specific period, at the end of which it is revised, taking into account new emphases, objectives and means. Experience confirms the usefulness of such a programme of action for catechesis. By defining certain common objectives it encourages various interests to work together with a common purpose. Thus realism should be the first characteristic of a programme of action, then simplicity, conciseness and clarity.

282.   Together with the programme of action—focused above all on workable options—many Episcopates prepare, at national level, catechetical materials of a orientational or reflective nature which provide criteria for an adequate and appropriate catechesis. These instruments are called by various names: *Catechetical Directory, Catechetical Guidelines, Basic Document, Reference Text,* etc. These are mainly addressed to those responsible for catechesis and to catechists. They clarify the concept of catechesis: its nature, object, tasks, contents, method and those to whom it is addressed. These directories or general guidelines prepared by Episcopal Conferences or published with their authority are obliged to follow the same process of elaboration and approval as catechisms. That is, such documents, before their publication, must be submitted to the Apostolic See for its approbation.[34] These catechetical guidelines are a source of great inspiration for catechesis in the local Churches and their elaboration is useful and recommended, because, amongst other things, they are an important point of reference for the formation of catechists. This kind of aid is closely and directly related to episcopal responsibility.

---

[34] Cf. DCG (1971) 117 and 134; PB 94.

Elaboration of instruments and didactic aids for catechetical activity

283. Along with those instruments dedicated to the orientation and general planning of catechetical activity (*analysis of the situation, plan of action, Catechetical Directory*), there are other instruments of more immediate use in catechetical activity. In the first place, mention must be made of *textbooks*,[35] which are placed directly in the hands of catechumens and those being catechized. Also helpful are the various catechetical *Guides* for both catechists and, in the case of the catechesis of children, for parents.[36] *Audio-visual* aids too are important in catechesis and appropriate discernment should be exercised in their use.[37] The basic criterion for these work aids should be that of twofold fidelity to God and to man, a fundamental principle for the whole Church. This implies an ability to marry perfect doctrinal fidelity with a profound adaptation to man's needs, taking into consideration the psychology of age and the socio-cultural context in which he lives.

---

[35] With regard to this ensemble of catechetical books *Catechesi Tradendae* notes: "one of the major features of the renewal of catechetics today is the rewriting and multiplication of catechetical books taking place in many parts of the Church. Numerous very successful works have been produced and are a real treasure in this service of catechetical instruction" (CT 49).
DCG (1971) 120 defines textbooks in the following way: "textbooks are aids offered to the Christian community that is engaged in catechesis. No text can take the place of a live communication of the Christian message; nevertheless, the texts do have great value in that they make it possible to present a fuller exposition of the witnesses of Christian tradition and of principles that foster catechetical activity".

[36] With regard to catechetical manuals DCG (1971) 121 indicates what they should contain: "an explanation of the message of Salvation (constant reference must be made to the sources and a clear distinction must be kept between those things which pertain to the faith and to the doctrine that must be held, and those things which are mere opinions of theologians); psychological and pedagogical advice; suggestions about methods".

[37] Cf. Part Three, chap. 2, *Social communication;* cf. DCG (1971) 122.

In short, catechetical aids must:

– be "linked with the real life of the generation to which they are addressed, showing close acquaintance with its anxieties and questionings, struggles and hopes"; [38]

– try "to speak meaingfully to this generation";[39]

– "really aim to give to those who use them a better knowledge of the mysteries of Christ, aimed at true conversion and a life more in conformity with God's will".[40]

Preparation of local catechisms: a direct responsibility of the episcopal ministry

284. Among the aids available to catechesis, catechisms excel all others.[41] Their importance derives from the fact that the message transmitted by them is recognized as authentic by the Pastors of the Church. If the Bishop presides over the general catechetical activity of a particular Church, it is also true that the publication of catechisms is a direct responsibility of the episcopal ministry. National, regional, or diocesan catechisms, drawn up in co-operation with catechetical workers, are ultimately the responsibility of the Bishops, who are catechists *par excellence* in the particular Churches.

In drawing up catechisms, the following two criteria must be carefully adhered to.

---

[38] CT 49b.
[39] *Ibid.*
[40] *Ibid.*
[41] The question of local catechisms has been dealt with in Part two, chap. II. Here we intend to present only some criteria for their elaboration. By the term "local catechisms" the present document refers to those catechisms which are proposed by particular Churches or by Episcopal Conferences.

a) perfect harmony with the *Catechism of the Catholic Church*: "a sure and authentic reference... particularly for preparing local catechisms"; [42]

b) due consideration for the norms and criteria for the presentation of the Gospel message contained in the *General Directory for Catechesis*, which is also a "standard of reference" [43] for catechesis.

285. The *"prior approbation of the Apostolic See"* [44] which is required for catechisms emanating from Episcopal Conferences—signifies that these are documents whereby the universal Church, in the differing socio-cultural contexts to which she is sent, proclaims and transmits the Gospel and "generates the particular Churches by manifesting herself in them".[45] The approbation of a catechism is a recognition of the fact that it is a text of the universal Church for a specific culture and situation.

---

[42] FD 3c.
[43] CT 50.
[44] DCG (1971) 119, 134; CIC 775 § 2; PB 94.
[45] CONGREGATION FOR THE DOCTRINE OF THE FAITH, *"Communionis Notio"* 9; *l.c.* 843.

CONCLUSION

286.   In formulating the present guidelines and directives every possible effort has been made to ensure that they are based on the teachings of the Second Vatican Council and on the subsequent interventions of the Church's Magisterium. Particular attention has, moreover, been given to the experience of ecclesial life among different peoples in the interim. In the light of fidelity to the spirit of God the requisite discernment has been exercised, always, however, with a view to the renewal of the Church and the service of evangelization.

287.   This new Directory is offered to all the Pastors of the Church, to their fellow workers and to catechists in the hope that it may serve as an encouragement in the service which the Church and the Holy Spirit entrusts to them, namely, fostering the growth of faith in those who believe. The guidelines, contained herein, are intended not only to clarify the nature of catechesis and the norms and criteria which govern this evangelizing ministry of the Church but to nurture, with the power of the word and the interior action of the Holy Spirit, the hope of those who labour in this privileged area of ecclesial activity.

288.   The effectiveness of catechesis is and always will be a gift of God, through the operation of the Spirit of the Father and the Son. St Paul, in his letter to the Corinthians, confirms this total dependence on the intervention of God when he writes: *"I planted, Apollos watered, but God gave the growth. So neither he who plants nor he who waters is anything, but only God who gives the growth"* (1 Cor 3:6-7).

Neither catechesis nor evangelization is possible without the action of God working through his Spirit.[1] In catechetical praxis neither the most advanced pedagogical techniques nor the most talented catechist can ever replace the silent and unseen action of the Holy Spirit.[2] "It is he who is in truth the protagonist of all the Church's mission";[3] it is he who is the principal catechist; it is he who is "the interior teacher" of those who grow in the Lord.[4] He is, in fact, "the principle inspiring all catechetical work and all who do this work".[5]

289.   May patience and trust abide in the spirituality of the catechist, since it is God himself who sows, gives growth, and brings to fruition the seed of his word, planted in good soil and tended with love. St Mark, the Evangelist, is alone in recounting the parable by which Jesus makes us to understand the stages, one after the other, whereby the scattered seed gradually and constantly develops: *"The Kingdom of God is as if a man should scatter seed upon the ground, and should sleep and rise night and day, and, the seed should sprout and grow, he knows not know. The earth produces of itself, first the blade, then the ear, then the full grain in the ear. But when the grain is ripe, at once he puts in the sickle, because the harvest has come"* (Mk 4:26-29).

290.   The Church, which has the responsibility of catechizing those who believe, invokes the Spirit of the Father and of the Son, begging him to give fruitfulness and interior strength to the toil which is everywhere undertaken for the growth of the faith and the fellowship of Our Saviour Jesus Christ.

[1] Cf. EN 75a.
[2] Cf. EN 75d.
[3] RM 21.
[4] Cf. CT 72.
[5] CT 72.

291. Today as ever, all labourers of catechesis, trusting in her intercession, turn to the Blessed Virgin Mary, who saw her Son grow "in wisdom, age and grace" (*Lk* 2,52). They find in her the spiritual model for carrying out and strengthening the renewal of contemporary catechesis, in faith, hope and love. Through the intercession of the "Virgin of Pentecost",[6] there is born in the Church a new power, generating sons and daughters in the faith and educating them toward the fullness of Christ.

His Holiness Pope John Paul II, on 11 August 1997, approved this present General Directory for Catechesis and authorized its publication.

✠ DARÍO CASTRILLÓN HOYOS
Archbishop Emeritus of Bucaramanga
Pro-Prefect

✠ CRESCENZIO SEPE
Titular Archbishop of Grado
Secretary

---

[6] CT 73.

THEMATIC INDEX

Numbers in this index correspond to those of the *General Directory for Catechesis.*
Numbers in bold type indicate fundamental texts.
Cf refers to related texts.